Selecting Training Methods

Stockport *College*
Of Further and Higher Education

The Business School

RESOURCE BASED LEARNING CENTRE

The Competent Trainer's Toolkit Series
by David G. Reay

1. *Understanding the Training Function*

2. *Planning a Training Strategy*

3. *Understanding How People Learn*

4. *Identifying Training Needs*

5. *Selecting Training Methods*

6. *Implementing Training*

7. *Evaluating Training*

Selecting Training Methods is the fifth 'tool' in the series. The first —
Understanding the Training Function — stands outside the training cycle. The rest,
including this book, deal with the cycle stage by stage, from planning your initial
strategy right through to evaluating the contribution training makes to the prosperity
of your organization.

All these books can be used on training courses or as aids to self-development.

Selecting Training Methods

DAVID G REAY

Kogan Page Ltd, London
Nichols Publishing Company,
New Jersey

First published in 1994

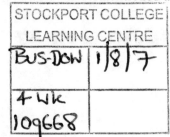

Kogan Page Limited
120 Pentonville Road
London N1 9JN

© OTSU Ltd 1994

Published in the United States of America by Nichols Publishing,
PO Box 6036, East Brunswick, New Jersey 08816

British Library Cataloguing in Publication Data

A CIP record of this book is available from the British Library.
ISBN: (UK) 0 7494 1286 0
ISBN: (US) 0-89397-425-0

Printed and bound in Great Britain by Biddles Ltd, Guildford and King's Lynn

Contents

Acknowledgements **6**

Introduction **7**
So What is *Selecting Training Methods* All About? *8*
Objectives *9* Training and Development Lead Body
Competences *10* Overview *12* Where to Start *14*
Where to Finish *15*

1 **Criteria for Selection — A Structured Approach** **16**
The Subject Matter *17* The Learners *20* Training
Resources *25* Organizational Expectations *29*
Summary *32*

2 **Group-Based Training Explained** **33**
Ground Rules *34* Learning through Spectating *35*
Learning through Contributing *40* Process Skills *49*
Summary *53*

3 **Side-by-Side Training Explained** **57**
Defining Side-by-Side Training *58* Developing an OJT
System — the Process *62* Summary *69*

4 **Text-Based Open Learning Explained** **72**
Defining Open Learning *73* What are the Benefits of
Open Learning Materials? *76* How 'Open' Should
Open Learning Be? *78* Two Different Types of Open
Learning *82* Summary *84*

5 **Technology-Based Training Explained** **87**
Development of Technology *88* Four Types of
Technology *89* Types of Programme Used *91* The
Challenge of New Technology *92* Summary *93*

6 **Discovery Learning Explained** **96**
Defining Discovery Learning *97* Three Approaches *97*
Summary *100*

7 **The Final Choice** **103**
Making Sure *104* Developmental Testing *106*
Evaluation *109* Summary *110* Conclusion *111*

Further Reading **112**

Acknowledgements

This series is to a large extent based on OTSU's experiences during the past decade. Because of this, so many people have been involved in its formulation that, it would be impossible to name them all. However, there are a number of people without whose help this series would not have seen the light of day.

I would like therefore to give my sincere thanks to Paul Leach for his constant support with writing, Adrian Spooner for his editing skill, Aidan Lynn for setting the series in motion, Jill Sharpe and Kathleen Gibson for design and desk-top publishing, Dorothy Reay and Amanda Froggatt for proof-reading and finally Dolores Black at Kogan Page who didn't mind flexible deadlines.

Introduction

Who chooses the training methods in your organization? The chances are that the choice is left to you the trainer, or to a small team within the training function, although there are of course organizations which prefer to regard training as a sub-set of personnel — in which case, a personnel officer will make the choice.

But how? In the experiences of my team and myself working in organizations across Europe and the USA, there are three methods — and one way which doesn't even count as a method at all. This non-method is simply 'trusting to luck': you ask someone to do some training for you and it doesn't matter what they do. They may close the whole section for a day or they may distribute diagrams; no one cares and of course, it won't do. The methods, in increasing order of effectiveness are: first, reacting to pressure — pressure from unsolicited mail or pressure from your trainees, it doesn't matter. You're looking for an idea, someone provides one and that's that. It may succeed or it may not. Second, there is the inheritance factor: you find yourself in position as a new trainer and just inherit the training methods from your predecessor. Again, these may or may not be effective, but we believe that there is always room for innovation and improvement. Third, there is the proactive option: making an informed choice of which training methods are best.

In theory, you can use any training method you choose to teach anybody anything. In practice, though, there are a whole range of criteria which should be applied to training methods before you can be sure that the ones you choose are right.

It is vital that you should choose the most appropriate method at every turn, because inappropriate methods lead to ineffective learning, dissatisfaction with your performance felt by trainees and those who pay the bills within your organization and, to cap it all, a detrimental effect on your organization's performance. While the overall tone of this book is of course positive, it is worth remembering the consequences of a wrong choice.

There are key questions which you must always answer satisfactorily if you're to be sure you've made the best choice. The questions arise in four main areas:

- cost — because there's no point selecting a training method you can't afford

- subject matter — because you can't, for example, teach surgery by text alone

- learning style — because certain learners respond better to some training methods than to others

- organizational objectives — because training methods which run counter to what the organization is trying to achieve can't succeed.

You will see more about the questions to ask as you read through this text.

So What is *Selecting Training Methods* All about?

Selecting Training Methods is all about ensuring that you choose the method of training which is going to be most effective in your situation. Theoretically, it's possible to teach anybody anything in any way. For example, customer relations can be taught by text, role-play, video, interactive video . . . it all depends on the constraints of your particular situation.

Effectiveness is ultimately measured by evaluation, and in the light of evaluation, training methods can be amended, discarded, adopted, or combined to make something both more effective and more appropriate. But where do you *start* from? *Selecting Training Methods* will enable you to make an informed judgement about which training methods are likely to succeed. This removes the need to 'have a stab at something' and then learn from what may be a very expensive mistake. Instead, you'll be able to figure out precisely what training method or combination of methods is most likely to succeed, and then adopt it.

You will look at the training method most regularly used and see what is involved in each one; this will enable you to identify the areas and situations where each is most likely to succeed; and from this point you will find it easier to select methods for your situation.

Objectives

By the time you have completed this book, you will be able to:

- describe accurately the areas in which the key questions relating to your choice of method arise

- put together a specification for the training methods which would be most effective in your organization

- describe the methodology, organizational framework, resource requirements, support structure and target audiences involved in group training, side-by-side training, text-based open learning, technology-based training and discovery learning.

- undertake a critical evaluation of the methods listed above in the context of your organization

- apply the needs-methods matrices contained in the book to the selection of training methods in your organization

- describe the aids and techniques necessary to make effective use of the training methods explained in this book.

Training and Development Lead Body Competences

Many trainers and training managers in the UK are actively seeking professional vocational qualifications, through the National Vocational Qualification route. There are competences at level 3 and level 4 of the NVQ in Training and Development for which you will be able to use this book as part of your portfolio of evidence.

I have prepared, on the following page, a matrix which matches a list of assignments in this book and the competences, published in autumn 1994, which appear in the scheme booklets provided by the awarding bodies. Simply tick off the numbered assignments as you do them. Then, when you've completed this book, you can include the book itself, together with any supporting documents you may create as you work through it, in your NVQ portfolio. The simple matching technique will allow your NVQ assessor easily to locate your evidence and match it against the relevant criteria. Each assignment goes towards meeting performance criteria outlined in the elements shown.

Assignment at end of chapter	The Assignment Counts as Evidence Towards these Elements						
1	A123	A131	A133	A212	B112	B211	B311
2 (Assignment 1)	B222	B312	B331	B332			
2 (Assignment 2)	B111	B112	B121	B122	B211	B221	
3 (Assignment 1)	B221	B222	B312	B322	B331	B332	C111
3 (Assignment 2)	B211	B122	B123	B221	B311		
4 (Assignment 1)	A211	D211	D212	D213			
4 (Assignment 2)	B111	B121	B211	B311	C113		
5 (Assignment 1)	B311	B321	MCI SM3		MCI 1 Unit 3		MCI 2 Unit 4
5 (Assignment 2)	B111	B121	B321				
6 (Assignment 1)	A212	A221	B211	B221	B222	B311	B312
	B331	B332	C111	C251	C252		
6 (Assignment 2)	B111	B121	B211				
7	A133	A211	A221	B111	B112	B121	B221
	B312	B322	B331	C272			

A123   Determine organizational aims and objectives for training and development

A131   Collect information for an organization's training and development needs analysis

A133   Specify organizational training and development needs

A211   Collect information from individuals on their learning requirements

A212   Identify and agree individuals' learning requirements

A221   Identify available learning opportunities

B111   Identify potential strategies for training and development in an organization

B112   Devise a strategy for training and development within an organization

B121   Select options for implement training and development objectives

B122   Develop a training and development implementation plan

B123   Prepare the implementation of the plan

B211   Select options for meeting learning requirements

B221   Identify options for training and development sessions

B222   Design training and development sessions for learners

B311   Design information technology (IT) based training materials

B312   Design training and development materials

B321   Agree requirements for information technology (IT) based training and development materials with clients

B322   Design Information Technology (IT) based training materials

B331   Prepare materials and facilities to support learning

B332   Develop materials to support learning

C111   Agree roles and resources with contributors

C113   Monitor and review the effectiveness of contributions

C251   Coach individual learners

C252   Assist individual learners to apply their learning

C272   Facilitate collaborative learning

D211   Collect evidence from individuals for non-competence based assessment

D212   Analyse evidence to form an assessment decision

D213   Provide feedback to individuals on the assessment decision

MCI 1 Unit 3   Recommend, monitor and control the use of resources

MCI 2 Unit 4   Secure effective resource allocation for activities and projects

MCI SM3   Contribute to the planning, monitoring and control of resources

Overview

This book is structured so that you can use it first of all to follow a logical path through the process of arriving at the correct decision concerning training methods, and second so that you can use it as an easily accessible work of reference at any time. You'll see that its division into discrete sections will make it easy for you to find any information you need.

Chapter 1 — Criteria for Selection — A Structured Approach

In this chapter, we encourage you to think about a range of questions which are designed to guide you towards appropriate responses to training needs in your organization. We shall not, however, at this stage be offering many answers — they will come later. The questions you look at will be structured into four areas:

- the subject matter
- the learners
- the training resources
- organizational expectations.

Chapter 2 — Group Training Explained

Group training being probably the most commonly practised type, we show you the difference between active learning and passive learning, and demonstrate how one or the other (or a combination) can meet some of your needs.

Chapter 3 — Side-by-Side Training Explained

Side-by-side training is one of the most natural training processes in the world. In this chapter we show how this sort of training encourages the learner to acquire new skills and habits in a practical way by practising them under the trainer's guidance and supervision.

Chapter 4 — Text-Based Open Learning Explained

In this chapter you will see we spend a fair amount of time defining open learning, both from a theoretical and a practical viewpoint, and clarifying the situation in which open learning will — or won't — be an effective training method.

Chapter 5 — Technology-Based Training Explained

The technology revolution has brought with it many opportunities for training. Computer-based training and interactive video are the longest established, but newcomers to the scene, CD-i and CD-ROM, are also worth assessing in the same light. You will see which methods will be most appropriate for your situation.

Chapter 6 — Discovery Learning Explained

Learning by discovery is, more than any other, 'nature's way', and this chapter shows how the natural drive to learn which is present in all of us can be harnessed to good effect. You'll also see whether it is likely to succeed in your situation.

Chapter 7 — The Final Choice

You need to be certain that the choice you're about to make is correct — so we recommend a developmental test to ensure that you are indeed making a wise selection. The steps of an accurate developmental test are described in this chapter.

Where to Start

The best place to start when seeking the best training method for your organization is with an accurate and detailed description of your own situation.

This surprisingly simple fact is often overlooked by trainers who are seduced by advertising or influenced by the success stories of others. To pick a medical metaphor, a medicine which cures one person may kill another with the same symptoms. The doctor's skill is to match the medicine to the patient — not to assume that all patients are the same.

So it is with you. Look to your own situation and find the training method which will fit it. Don't force your situation into a training method which may stifle it.

Where to Finish

Finish with an evaluation. The final tool in this series — *Evaluating Training* — will help; but remember that successful training will change your situation, perhaps so radically that you may need different training methods to address the new, changed situation.

If you feel that this implies that there is no end to training — in other words, that you don't actually 'finish' anywhere — then you're right. You should look on the evaluation as the finish only of one of the training cycles, which will be immediately succeeded by another on a higher plane.

Chapter 1

Criteria for Selection — A Structured Approach

When you're selecting a training method, you need to ask questions about that method. You need to know that it's right for **you** — in **your** situation. Faced with this need, it is perhaps tempting to ask questions as soon as they pop into your head: what will it cost? how long will it take?

The risks of the spontaneous approach is that you will overlook an important question which ought to be asked, and that you will, as a consequence, end up with an inappropriate selection. To ensure that this does not happen, we have designed a structure which you can use to question **any** method of training, and which will enable you to arrive with confidence at a decision you can rely on. The structure divides the questions you should ask into four areas.

This chapter is fairly detailed and deals with those four areas:

- the subject matter to be trained in
- the learners in your organization
- the training resources at your disposal
- organizational expectations.

By the time you've finished this chapter, you should be able to:

- state what is contained in each of those areas in sufficient detail to enable you to define your own situation in terms of those areas.

Without wishing to imply any order of importance or priority, we will deal with the areas in the order they appear above. It could be that in your situation the priority order is precisely the reverse of the one which appears here. You will be able to address this point for yourself as you progress.

The Subject Matter

That which is taught and learnt generally comes under three broad headings.

Think about everything you've ever learnt or picked up at home, at school and at work and then identify the three broad headings here.

-
-
-

The three broad headings are:

- knowledge
- skills
- attitudes.

Knowledge, Skills, Attitudes

Knowledge may be **pure knowledge**, which the learner is expected simply to **acquire,** or **applied knowledge**, which the learner must be able to **apply** to practical situations.

Skills, on the other hand, require **practice** to develop or perfect, and **attitudes** involve the way people **feel** about a job.

Case Study

Sarah Martin had been a senior operative in a large government department for years when the opportunity came to move into training.

When she arrived at the training department, she was delighted to see that a large computer-based training (CBT) initiative was under way and about to be launched. This programme enabled operatives to work their computer terminals more quickly and to take advantage of enhanced facilities offered by changes to the system. This would lead to customer requests being handled more swiftly . . . and that was the plan.

With her years in the office, Sarah knew that there was more to the problem than could be solved with a round of systems simulation training. This was skills focused, and while the people needed skills, they needed more.

Many people were working slowly either because they lacked basic knowledge, or they didn't know what to do with it. You can't process a claim form properly without knowing what it's about. So, they needed pure and applied knowledge. But more important than skills and knowledge was **attitude** training. Sarah knew that many people in her office didn't relate to the customers — the public at large — at all. They didn't feel the need to attend to the customer's affairs with any urgency; they weren't bothered.

It followed that the staff weren't motivated to learn knowledge and acquire skills, because they couldn't see the need. Sarah pressed for and was given the opportunity to take staff through a customer awareness package of her own devising. Once changed attitudes were in place, knowledge and skills soon followed.

Your first question must therefore focus on the extent to which knowledge, skills and attitudes are an issue in your situation. A fresh look at all of your training provision to see which areas are currently being addressed could be worthwhile!

Is the Subject Debatable?

The next issue to study is the outcome of your training. In the simplest terms, sometimes you're trying to get across that there is:

- only one right answer.

Other times you're giving a very different message:

- there is **never** only one right answer.

Clearly one training method alone is unlikely to convey both these ideas. Where **one** right answer is required, debate can be minimized. Where an open mind is called for, debate should be maximized.

Another situation where debate (or lack of it) is crucial is this:

- is the aim of training to **standardize** methods or procedures?
- or is the aim to develop **better solutions**?

Standardization requires little discussion, but the quest for something better often benefits from the exchange of ideas between people of very differing views.

If you're already starting to think that group discussion (at one extreme) and, say, a video-tape for individual use (at the other) are very different, but that each is strong in its own way, then good. This text is having the desired effect.

General or Specific?

In certain circumstances, trainees need to learn general techniques they can apply to a range of problems. For example, trainees preparing to man the reception desk need to know how to demonstrate calmness under pressure, knowledge of their environment, and the ability to communicate clearly and sympathetically with a range of people. The neurosurgeon, however, needs particular answers to specific questions, and skills to apply in particular situations.

By way of a summary of what we've said about the subject matter, here are the three key issues displayed in a part of a diagram which we'll build up as we go along.

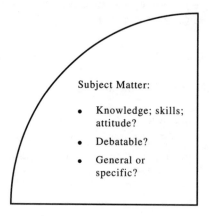

Subject Matter:

- Knowledge; skills; attitude?
- Debatable?
- General or specific?

Now it's time to move onto the next area of the chart.

The Learners

We've worked with the research and development departments of multinational chemical and engineering companies. Trainers in these situations are able to say that all their people learn in the same way. They're all from a research background. They all understand the value of experiments and recording results. These learners are homogeneous. But are yours?

Learning Styles

According to Alan Mumford and Peter Honey in their *Manual of Learning Styles* — which we refer to extensively with their kind permission in *Understanding How People Learn* — learners are classified under four headings:

- activists
- reflectors
- theorists
- pragmatists.

Which are you — and what makes you say so? Answer in this box.

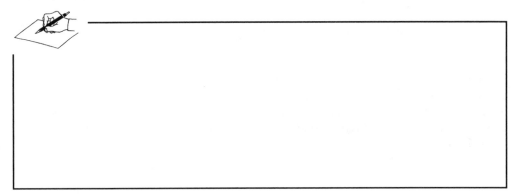

See how your description of yourself compares to our four brief outlines below.

The activist

Activists are always keen to have a go. You can expect them to be impetuous, impatient, untroubled at the thought of getting something wrong, open-minded and flexible. These are people who will not baulk at being asked to do something new or outside their normal routine. As a trainer, you might find yourself wincing at the prospect of enabling people like this to learn. How can you avoid being brushed aside as an irrelevance? *Understanding How People Learn* (book 3 in this series) explains this area in greater detail.

The reflector

Reflectors tend by nature to be cautious, careful and methodical. They're good at listening to others and will rarely jump to conclusions. Many trainers will enjoy having these people in their training sessions, because they bring judicious insights about the work they've been doing and criticize themselves constructively.

The theorist

Theorists tend to be rational and logical, and enjoy working with models which interpret their experience. They are disciplined in their approach to learning, and have the ability to ask objective questions. Their objectivity stems from their aptitude to distance themselves from their work. They take what they do, turn it into ideas, and work with these ideas in an abstract way. They are good people to have in a discussion because of the interesting sidelights they can cast on the subject under discussion.

The pragmatist

Pragmatists are planners; they are practical and down to earth. They enjoy nothing more than actually trying things out and making them work. They seek early opportunities to experiment with applications, and if you have them on a course, they'll be keen for it to finish so they can get back to the workplace and try one or two things out.

Learning Experience

It makes a great difference to the effectiveness of a piece of training if the method used coincides with another method successfully used by that learner before. It follows therefore that you need the answers to two questions:

1. What sort of training have my learners had before? — and don't forget to include broad general education here
2. Did they respond well or badly to it?

As regards the type of training your people may have had, the most accurate and reliable way of finding out is of course to ask them. Failing this, and as a rough guide, you could ask yourself:

- are they graduates, used to learning from books?
- are they practical people, happiest learning by doing?
- are they school-leavers, used to working in groups in a classroom?

As regards the success or otherwise of the training, again, asking is the most effective way of finding out. Otherwise, you may have records in your department. In the case of school-leavers, the calibre of their examination results will indicate the enthusiasm with which they responded to the teaching they received.

Numbers

The number of learners in the target group is often the deciding factor in the choice of training method. We could be a little cynical and say that because it is the most easily measured in the whole equation it is the one which is most frequently used. Practically, however, numbers are a very important consideration, You're not going to commission a video with a cast of thousands for the benefit of one individual. Nor are you going to get a subject expert to coach hundreds of individuals one-to-one.

Where are the Learners?

Trainers whose learners are situated in isolation at branches on the east coast and the west, as well as all parts north, south and in between, will out of necessity find themselves contemplating different training methods from those whose trainees are all centrally located, maybe in one office or department. The situation becomes even more complicated if there is an essential need for training to be absolutely consistent — which is our next point.

Are the Training Needs Consistent?

In a situation where the training is non-debatable, as might be the case where employees have to become familiar with new payroll arrangements, then consistency is vital, no matter how widely dispersed the people may be. Additionally, you may need to consider whether or not all your trainees are starting from the same base.

Case Study

Sam Bullevant learnt a major lesson when he organized his first conference. He visited people from all the branches and, in an effort to ensure the conference would be appropriate for everyone, he invited people on the same pay-grade.

His mistake was to overlook the different levels of experience the people had had of the particular topic in hand. For some, it was completely new, and they soon became disenchanted with the whole affair. For others, the initial speeches at the conference were all too familiar, and they made their feelings known not only to Sam but also to the speakers at the conference. It was all very embarrassing.

Sam, it goes without saying, was much more specific with his joining instructions next time he organized a conference.

What are the Learners' Expectations?

In some ways, learners' expectations are governed by their experiences. So, as we implied earlier, if they have had a poor experience of one method of training and you offer them more of the same, then you can expect resistance.

But there are other factors which might influence learner expectations. For example, you yourself might have made claims in some of your publicity material. You might have promised hands-on, practical material. If this turns out not to be forthcoming, then you can expect more than resistance. People will 'vote with their feet' and just leave you to it.

You should also consider the following issues:

- will the learners adapt easily to something they may not have tried before?
- will they need any extra help and support?
- are they motivated?
- will they feel threatened?

Any of these, if overlooked, could lead to your choosing an inappropriate method. Consider just one example: you conclude that for a piece of training which involves a complicated decision-tree method with only one acceptable outcome, a CBT programme would be ideal. You should not overlook the fact that people may need:

- special dispensation to leave their work-station to go to an appropriate terminal to work the CBT

- guidance in how to access the program, load the program, escape from the program . . . the technical side of things, in other words, may give cause for concern.

To summarize what we've said about the learner, we can prepare them to be included in the diagram.

The Learners:

- Learning styles?
- Learning experience?
- Numbers?
- Where are they located?
- Consistent needs?
- Expectations?

You're now ready to move on to our third area: resources.

Training Resources

It is possible to arrive at the perfect decision concerning your learners and your subject only to find that you can't resource it. There are obvious examples to pick on — CBT where there are no computers, and the like. This common situation, where you've identified the ideal solution, but you can't deliver it, can be avoided if you use a methodical approach. Ask yourself these questions, and you'll get the information you require.

1. What Training Skills and Experience Can You Call On?

Remembering that group training is the most common in the world — have you and your team experience in the latest techniques? Or are there still people in your team who point at the blackboard with a stick, and then, if people don't respond, can only call them back in to repeat the process?

In practical terms, you need to think very early on — who can deliver this course? Or — alternatively — who can write this book? — or make this video? There are, however, pressing reasons why this 'who' question should not be your very first. List those reasons here.

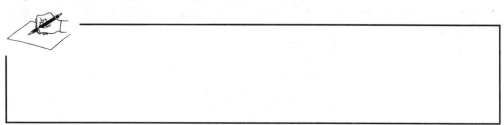

The most pressing reason is this:

- asking 'who' first of all is to switch the focus away from the learner to the provider. It becomes all too easy to ask, not, 'what do they need' but, 'what can we give them?'

Case Study

Ben Jolliffe Associates were specialists in open learning. Their early clients were no trouble to them; they all needed and were pleased to receive open learning. However, the trouble started when Ben began to propose open learning solutions to problems which didn't really have open learning solutions at all, solely on the grounds that Ben Jolliffe Associates were able to provide open learning.

Ben's client base soon evaporated.

You must avoid falling into that trap — but the question 'who' remains valid. You can't assign an in-house open learning solution to a problem if no one has ever done that sort of thing before. You can't expect people to deliver lectures who have never lectured before.

Assignment:

On a separate piece of paper create a grid to show who you can call on, and what the training experiences of each person are.

2. How Easily Can You Develop New Resources?

Your grid might have revealed a potential gap; at the very least it will have revealed limitations. Let us explain.

If you compare your skills and experience grid to your current training commitment, you may discover that people are down to deliver material in a way that they're not used to or not happy with. The training will occur, but it might not be as effective as possible. This situation — where you can't cover what you're committed to — is a **gap**.

Limitations are spotted when you look for ways in which you might expand and develop. For example, a course along the lines of discovery learning might suggest itself, but you reject it; there's no one you can call on to do that sort of thing effectively.

Faced with gaps and limitations, trainers react differently — according to temperament, of course — but also according to the situation. For some, it is easy to develop their people. There is a budget for trainer-training and it needs to be used. For others, the solution is, in the short term, to restrict the output of the training function in the light of available skills, but to press for a development budget at the earliest opportunity.

The situation is very similar when you assess your other resources. Some trainers can expand readily. Others have to bide their time until they can negotiate a budget.

3. Is Location an Issue?

If you're training in an organization with sites spread all over the country, there are a few simple answers to these questions:

- who can you call on?

- what resources are available?

- how can they be developed?

The administration can be complicated — the sheer amount of the information concerning who is doing what, when and with whom can be overwhelming. Fundamental questions have to be asked:

- is the focus of the training to be central, with identical courses being run on different sites?

- is the training department better split into autonomous units, relating to one policy-making nerve-centre?

- is each site to become a 'centre of excellence' for one specific subject area?

The answers to these questions will influence your choice of training methods. Where identical courses are run on two or more sites, a method must be found which guarantees a high level of consistency of message, such as open learning. Where centres of excellence are chosen, the one-to-one skills of subject experts may come to the fore. And, where training departments have a degree of autonomy, you, as co-ordinator may find yourself called upon to compare and contrast different methods and make recommendations.

4. Are Time Constraints an Issue?

Some training methods take longer to implement than others. Diaries permitting, you can organize a lecture at fairly short notice, but you can't commission a video and expect to see it on the screen next week. It's a good training method, but it takes time.

To summarize what you've seen about training resources, here are the main points in another quarter of the diagram we're building up.

Training Resources:

- What skills or experience can you call on?
- Can you develop new resources?
- Location?
- Time?

Organizational Expectations

Does your organization have any pre-conceived ideas about what training ought to be and do? Write them in here.

Our experience indicates that there are three situations in which an organization's ideas can influence your choice of method:

1. the organization has its 'preferred methods'
2. the organization has specific objectives
3. certain methods of assessment and evaluation are insisted on.

You should take these in turn.

1 Preferred Method

There are many reasons why certain training styles develop and hold sway in an organization for years. One — a very common one, at that — is when senior colleagues recall their own training with wistfulness and rose-coloured spectacles. '"Chalk and talk", — that's the way to do it! It was good enough for me . . . '. Obtaining a flipchart and pens is a major concession wrung from these people — so you must realize that flying in the face of intractable opposition is not always the best way. Instead, we recommend that you:

-   build up a reputation as a thoughtful, successful trainer before you attack any really ingrained myths and prejudices
-   persist in seeking the benefits of any new approaches, which means:
    -   explaining
    -   describing
    -   getting trainees to give feedback
    -   providing reliable evaluation data.

2 The Organization Has Specific Objectives

Your organization will have established its own objectives. These will allow you to plan a logical learning sequence, starting with basic concepts, and anticipate the types of learning necessary.

3. Certain Methods of Assessment and Evaluation are Insisted On

You will have to make sure, in selecting appropriate training methods and techniques, that you also select the appropriate tests and assessment techniques that your organization requires. The logical sequence of objectives provides an equally logical sequence of content, methods and assessment.

Let's add the information on organizational expectations to the other criteria we've examined to complete the circle.

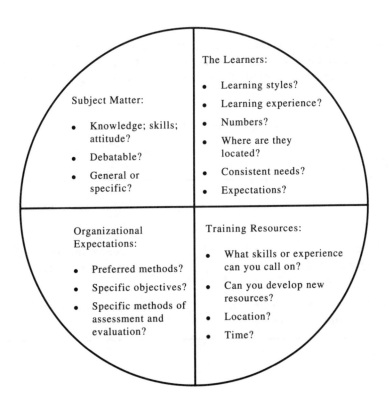

The Learners:

- Learning styles?
- Learning experience?
- Numbers?
- Where are they located?
- Consistent needs?
- Expectations?

Subject Matter:

- Knowledge; skills; attitude?
- Debatable?
- General or specific?

Organizational Expectations:

- Preferred methods?
- Specific objectives?
- Specific methods of assessment and evaluation?

Training Resources:

- What skills or experience can you call on?
- Can you develop new resources?
- Location?
- Time?

Summary

This chapter has dealt with four areas in which criteria for judging training methods arise. These were:

- the subject matter — knowledge, skills and attitudes
- the learners — their learning styles and experiences
- the training resources — trainer's skills, materials available
- organizational expectations.

Using these areas throughout the next chapters, you are now ready to consider different training methods and compare them against specific criteria. Then you will be able to select the training methods which will be most effective for your organization.

The next chapter deals with many different approaches under the heading of group training.

Assignment:

1. *Write out your own summary of the four areas you've looked at. Note down for each any questions you need to ask concerning your organization.*

2. *Finally, describe your organization in each of these areas, and prioritize the areas appropriately.*

Group-Based Training Explained

For many people, training **is** group-based; it's the only method they are used to, it's the only one they're in any way geared up for, and it is what the organization expects.

We're not in the business of overturning methods and ideas just because they're popular or common. We positively recommend group-based training for many situations, as you'll see in this chapter. What you'll also see is that under the broad banner of group-based training, there are many different methods, each with its own advantages, and, of course, each will have its own limitations.

By the time you've finished this chapter, you will be able to:

- tell which group-based learning methods involve learners as spectators, and which as contributors
- identify 9 group-based training methods and list the advantages and limitations of each
- define the circumstances in which group-based training is most likely to have optimum effect in your organization.

You should begin your exploration of group training with a few ground rules.

Ground Rules

The first ground rule to remember relates to learning theory. In book 3 of this series we demonstrated that there is no such thing as teaching. The skill of the teacher or the trainer is that they enable learning to take place. The learning process is largely a matter of what goes on inside the learner's head.

There are teachers and trainers who overlook this point to the detriment of their performance at work, and we can understand how this happens, although we do not really sympathize. Trainers are tempted to think that because they've presented something clearly, it has been learnt clearly. This may not be the case, however. It's true that poor presentation will thwart anyone's attempts to learn, but even so, a good presentation does not guarantee good learning. In a phrase, ground rule 1 is:

- **involve** the learners.

Only if you involve them — rather than merely present to them — can you enable them to learn.

Ground rule 2 is:

- **vary** the diet.

Given that each individual learner has a limited concentration span, you cannot expect him or her to spend all day involved in, say, a demonstration or a role-play or any other single activity.

What makes it even more pressing to offer the group a change of activity is that all the learners are different. Each will respond to a different method more or less positively, and the more methods you use (up to a certain point) the more likelihood there is that everyone will profit from some part of your provision. Don't go over the top, though. There are nearly a dozen different techniques examined in this chapter alone. Use them all before lunchtime and you'll give the impression of being manic and distracted!

This chapter is going to explore different training methods you can use if you decide to employ group training in your organization. We begin with training methods where the learners spectate rather than contribute.

Learning through Spectating

Lectures

We advise extreme caution when you decide to include lectures among your training methods. Lectures — even delivered well — offer minimal opportunity for learner involvement, and consequently minimal opportunity to learn. Your audience will switch off after a few minutes. Poor lectures are a complete waste of time.

Within the training event you may call a 'lecture' it is possible to include video presentations, demonstrations, role-play, discussion — but these are separate methods. A 'lecture' made up of lots of methods in an appropriate mix may provide the combination of involvement and variety essential to effective learning. An hour's solid lecturing will most certainly not.

Advantage:

- the low costs of delivering a lecture — particularly in-house.

Limitations:

- a straight lecture leaves the learners uninvolved: anyone can learn to look attentive while staying 'switched off'. Even listening hard and note-taking are inactive in the sense that little thought is required, so little learning takes place
- at best we switch our attention on and off. Six minutes is thought to be the maximum time during which most people absorb and retain information
- less than 20 per cent of information is retained one week later
- a lecture is highly dependent on the trainer's interpersonal skills and techniques if it is to achieve anything at all.

Videos and Films

Both of these training methods are essentially spectator-orientated. It's time that they offer a diverse range of opportunity, enabling learners to reach impossible locations, get into moving parts, sit in on a 'whole' experience and while this is entertaining, there is no guarantee of **learning**. Even the most sophisticated learner looks forward to a film as a 'break' from learning — but it's **not**, or, rather, it shouldn't be.

If you decide to use a video or film:

- make sure you will be able to see it first, and check that it's relevant

- don't rely on it utterly to deliver your training for you

- ensure you have time and opportunity to build it into the training as you would any learning aid

- ensure that you can involve learners in the video or film. You should brief learners before the viewing; provide a short list of questions or points to look for. Don't expect them to write much during the viewing, but to be able to discuss the points or questions afterwards.

Advantages:

- good examples are lively and interesting and motivate people to watch

- consistent message can be delivered in different times and places

- perfect for showing processes

- can be powerful attitude changer with emotional appeal.

Limitations:

- often difficult to relate to everyday work

- no opportunity for interaction with the equipment or involvement of any sort

- soon becomes dated
- poor examples are a real turn-off.

We would sum up our comments on video by saying that films and videos are a useful tool to have at your disposal, but we would not advise you to use them on your major training input.

Demonstrations

A demonstration is a presentation which illustrates a task, a procedure, or the use of equipment, showing the learner how to do it, but just watching an expert at work isn't enough to guarantee learning or anything like it. Demonstrations only guarantee learning if the learners have a chance to **try it themselves immediately**.

It will suit any type of objective with specific:

- procedure
- skill

   or

- reflex behaviour.

Now let us consider the advantages and limitations of this method.

Advantages:

- learners have the chance to observe carefully and learn key points (often dangers) **before trying themselves**
- learners can clarify their own learning needs during the demonstration, and feel motivated to develop the same skills as the trainer
- it enables the trainer to monitor individual performance and correct errors quickly, before they become established patterns of behaviour.

Limitations:

- none unique to demonstrations. Slower or less motivated learners may need to have the demonstration repeated, perhaps individually before trying it themselves.

Now you should consider the preparations that need to be made before giving a demonstration.

Preparing for a demonstration:

- plan to keep it short and simple, with as few key points as possible. Practise slow movement to illustrate the points

- ensure steps are logical — and will seem logical to learners

- start from basic concepts and build skills through several demonstrations if necessary, **each followed by practice**

- double-check your objectives: are they simply 'how to' ones, or will they include 'why' and 'when'? Will your learners know that?

- will everyone be able to see the demonstration clearly? If not, what will they do? Can you set some learners another task while each demonstration takes place?

- plan your introduction to the demonstration carefully. Use questions to check that learners know the concept, skills and context before the demonstration begins.

Interim Review

This is a suitable point for a review, because the methods you've seen so far have all been predominantly spectator-based; and those to follow are predominantly contributor-based.

Treating trainees purely as spectators does not enable learning to take place, so if you're planning:

- lectures

- film and video shows
- demonstrations

you must remember to restrict the 'now-hear-this' element to a minimum and to introduce periods of learner contribution into the scheme of things.

It could be that even these modest concessions in favour of learner involvement run counter to your organization's expectations — and organizational expectations, as we discussed in Chapter 1, are a key area in which criteria arise which will affect your selection of training methods.

What would you do if your organization expressed a strong preference for pure 'spectator'-training? Write your answer in here.

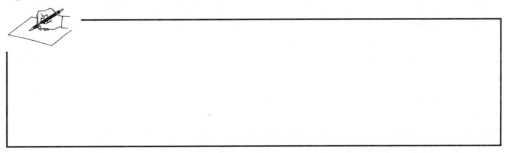

In extreme cases of organizational pressure, of course you would have to give in to demands. But we would recommend that it should become a key part of your strategy to change your organization's perceptions of what works in training and what doesn't. This could involve you in presentations to your customers before new training initiatives. It will certainly involve you in careful evaluation of new initiatives (if you get the go-ahead) so that you can prove your case.

If your organization is completely hide-bound — not to say fossilized — in its old-fashioned approach to training, only you can decide whether you want to face the challenge of changes, acquiesce, or move on to another job.

To resume a more positive vein, however, we'd like to show you some key points concerning other group-based training activities, so that you may select or reject them with confidence. The following 'set' occupies the rest of this chapter, and they all require learner contribution.

Learning through Contributing

Contribution involves learners in some kind of activity which leads to learning. This may be between:

- individual learners and the group leader
- the learner and a task
- various members of the group.

This opens the door to a wide variety of learning methods which, if used properly, can lead to the excitement and stimulation of active group learning. Let us start with describing three active learning methods which are dependent on the interaction between people:

- brainstorming
- discussions
- role play

We will examine the features and benefits of each and then consider the circumstances in which they would be most effective.

Brainstorming

Brainstorming is a group exercise which is a useful way to encourage lateral thinking. It provides a pool of ideas to open up topics, explore attitudes or help in problem-solving.

The basic rules:

- go for quantity: as many ideas as possible
- note every idea without judgement — the odder or funnier the better
- do it quickly: leave any reviewing or commenting until later.

Running a brainstorm session:

With people who are unused to brainstorming, try the following approach:

1. define the problem or issue as a simple question or statement

2. give people a couple of minutes to note down their private thoughts first

3. go round each person in turn, asking for one word or short phrase. Transcribe their exact words on a flipchart without comment

4. make it clear that anyone who can't think of something is entitled to simply say 'pass': minds quickly go blank if someone else has just made the same point

5. keep going round until several people say 'pass', then take any remaining ideas from anyone.

Follow up the brainstorm by using the flipchart in some way, perhaps to categorize ideas, or prioritize points.

Advantages:

- it requires a high level of involvement from all trainees
- it provides opportunity to 'speak your mind' in a safe environment
- it gets everyone thinking about the whole subject
- it's quick — rapid feedback for learners.

Disadvantages:

- it can drift off the point and develop the wrong point
- it's an uncritical process, so inappropriate ideas may get through
- it evades nuances and finer, more subtle points
- it can be loud and anarchic.

Discussions

This is both a method in itself and a technique built into many methods. It may take the form of a whole group of learners together, or several small groups or syndicates. In small groups, four to six participants are ideal, giving everyone space to make contributions and encouraging quieter people to take part. The trainer may lead the discussion or allow small groups to organize themselves.

The types of learning objective for discussion groups are to do with:

- changing attitudes
- comparing experience
- contrasting knowledge
- exploring applications

  or

- developing commitment.

Write down two advantages and two limitations in using the discussion method.

Advantages:

- contributions are pooled
- there is a high level of participation, which can mean in turn readiness to learn and change
- there is a sense of equal status which improves self-worth and image
- misconceptions can be identified and corrected.

Limitations:

- the larger the group is the less the participation by each member
- difficulties can arise if the leader is unskilled in group work or leadership, or some members dominate or feel under threat in any way.

We hope it's clear from the above points that there's no one kind of discussion, and no one way to plan a discussion. The leader's role is to stimulate group members to think for themselves and to express their thoughts. It is certainly not an easy alternative, and should be planned with the same clear objectives as those set for any other method.

Role Play

This is a method in which the learner practises a face-to-face situation that represents real life. By practising roles in the safety of the learning situation, each learner gains insights into their own and others' behaviour or needs.

What are the types of learning objective?

Role play can be used for any objective concerned with attitude or interpersonal skills development.

Advantages:

- a useful transitional stage between theory and practice
- an active learning experience which involves the whole group in a variety of tasks and enables them to draw their own conclusions and formulate their own ideas
- an opportunity for each learner to get feedback on their behaviour from the rest of the group, and to compare their behaviour with others in the group.

Limitations:

- if the preparation is less than meticulous, irrelevant and distracting points may arise

- even the thought of role play upsets some people, and they can't participate.

It would be up to the trainer to dispel such fears by providing a supportive environment.

Features of role play

Basic role play includes one learner who is given a role task representative of their work situation; for example, a 'college tutor' meeting a student at induction, a 'supervisor' dealing with a shop-floor complaint. A second learner acts the part of a client with whom the learner deals.

Both people are briefed on their task and the situation before enacting it. Afterwards they reflect on the situation, their feelings and what they have learned.

This basic role play 'pair' can be adapted in a number of ways:

- the whole group can be divided into pairs practising together

- the group can be divided into threes, the third person acting as observer and reporting back afterwards

- the whole group might observe one pair at a time

- the basic 'pair' can be adapted: several learners enacting a shared role task such as team-work, or several 'actors' representing different clients. The client might be a real person invited in to take part in the role play.

Preparing for a role play

Brief the learners, 'actors' and observers separately on their tasks. The learner or learners need to know the context of the role play in their work, but may be unaware of the personality which the actor will be assuming.

Those who are 'actors' need more briefing on the person they are playing: their history, feelings and state of mind for example — if these are relevant! Observers, too, need guidance: what are they looking for? How will they give feedback? Suggest that all feedback be given in a positive, sympathetic manner.

The threat people can feel from taking part in role play will be greatly reduced if everyone in turn has a chance to practise the role.

We've grouped brainstorming, discussion and role play together because of their dependence on **people**. You don't learn much from arguing with yourself and there's not much realism in role playing to a mirror!

Our next three learning methods are different because here people learn primarily from the activity and independently from each other.

We will consider the following three methods:

- case-studies
- exercises
- simulations.

Here, the main learning takes place as learners attempt to apply their own knowledge and experience to problem situations, either practical or written-up as narrative, which require actions or solutions. So, in principle, you can learn from a case study, an exercise or a simulation totally on your own. Indeed, that's the way some professional examinations and computer simulations work. We feel that's rather a waste, though. Used as an approach to group learning, there's tremendous benefit in sharing and debating ideas and experiences which would be relevant to solving the problem. You can add more excitement by making the exercise competitive between groups.

Case Studies

A case study is a story which documents a situation or event involving characters. It may be either:

- **a case illustration**, describing decisions that characters made in the given situation. In this case, the learners' task could be to criticize the decisions, or identify faults or mistakes

- **a case problem**, posing the problem facing characters. Learners could be asked to analyse data, make their own decisions — and defend their reasons. There need not be only one 'right' answer.

The types of learning objectives

Here we are concerned with:

- analytical thinking
- decision making and problem solving
- application of theory, procedure or attitude to 'real life'.

Can you think of some possible advantages and limitations for this method?

Advantages:

- case study topics can — indeed should — relate closely to learners' working environment and knowledge, giving them the chance to review typical situations in a relaxed atmosphere that's free from pressure and stress

- it is a method which involves feelings and attitudes as well as skills and knowledge.

Limitations:

- one of the limitations in making your own case study is that the initial preparation can be costly and time-consuming. But once tried and tested a good case study may be used many times and is cheap to run.

Case studies can be presented in the following ways:

- print — a main 'document', possibly supported by graphs, diagrams or other useful data
- video or film
- narrators — who may be people reporting their own real story, or actors.

Exercises

This term is often used as a generic description of any task or activity a learner is asked to perform. It may involve individual or small group work, many sorts of writing and/or discussion, and meet many types of learning objective.

Key features are that learners are asked to do *something* (explore, discuss, answer, complete, argue, compare, try — and so on), and then *review* (analyse, self-assess, deduce, build . . .)

Even if using exercises as some form of learner assessment, build in as much learner self-assessment or group assessment as you can.

Advantages:

- exercises set by the tutor are excellent for reinforcement of what has been learnt
- they guarantee at least some level of trainee involvement
- if designed carefully, they can reproduce in-company application of what has been learnt.

Limitations:

- exercises can be seen as the sole reason for doing the course; success in the exercise is equated with success in the course and successful application in practice
- exercises can tend to dominate events.

Simulations

These can take many forms:

- group simulations in which a number of people take on roles, plan strategies, enact meetings, put arguments, and so on
- individual exercises with simulators such as aeroplane flight controls, computers or interactive video, into which the learner feeds decisions and messages, and to which the device responds.

They provide a more complex 'real-time' learning experience. This method draws on both case study and role play techniques to create an ongoing situation which represents real life decisions, choices and interactions.

You can choose the type of learning objective you require. Choices can be made to do with attitude, behaviour, reflex skills, knowledge, etc. Then you can *follow through* the implications of that choice, whether it concerns connecting cables or negotiating with a trade union or management.

Advantages:

- simulations give a rich learning experience in which learners discover for themselves the importance of principles, rules or values
- they can be used to synthesize or bring together different types of learning into a whole, realistic form
- they enable learners to make mistakes without damaging real equipment — or people.

Limitations:

- most high technology simulators are very expensive to buy-in or hire

- group simulation exercises are expensive and time-consuming to prepare. They need all the background information of case studies, and more scene-setting than role play.

Process Skills

Before we leave this chapter we must also consider two process skills which your training team must possess and which are crucial to the success of group learning:

- questioning
- reviewing.

Questioning

Questioning is less a method than a technique central to any method — or any aspect of the trainer's many roles.

Traditionally questions were used to check learners' understanding or knowledge as a form of assessment by the trainer. Effective learner-centred training uses questioning in many more ways with these advantages.

Advantages:

- stimulate thinking and awaken interest
- explore relevant experience and skills or knowledge
- involve more people in the discussion
- encourage active learning.

Limitations:

- effective questioning has no limitations.

If your questioning is restricting the learning of the group, then your questioning is ineffective.

Effective questioning depends on using a variety of types of question, and avoiding or limiting the use of others. For example, use:

- **open questions** to help learners explore issues or ideas and think for themselves
- **closed questions** (needing one-word or short-phrase answers) only to gather quick facts
- **redirected questions** to reflect one learner's question back to the whole group
- **pick-up questions** to refer to a previous contribution by someone and to develop the point further (often useful when a quiet person's comment has been overlooked by the group)
- **direct questions** (to one individual) as little as possible. They make others relax attention, and the targeted one feels 'put on the spot'. However, they can be useful at particular times, perhaps to draw in someone new in a heated debate, for example!

Reviewing

This is a technique by which the trainer halts a particular session and encourages learners to reflect on, or review, the **process** or **the learning points** of what they have just done or discussed. The focus should be on what the learners can learn for themselves from previous tasks or events.

The trainer cannot **tell** learners the important things they should identify from what has happened. Rather he or she should use questioning techniques to **draw out** their own feelings or discoveries and encourage participation.

Advantages:

Effective reviews enable learners to:

- better understand their own feelings and behaviour and those of others
- explore their motivations and blocks to learning
- take on ownership of the learning process
- become more independent.

Limitations:

- to be successful, reviews depend on learners trusting each other and the trainer
- the trainer needs to ask the right questions, make use of the answers and avoid stretching the discussion.

Reviewing progress involves the systematic checking of whether individual objectives are being achieved and whether they are still relevant. The effective use of different methods requires progress to be reviewed regularly.

Specifically the benefits of reviewing are that:

- objectives remain relevant
- activities contribute to achieving the overall plan

- the learners retain direction in working towards their objectives

- the support, training and resources needed are identified

- the learner's appraisal will be backed by regular and consistent evidence.

Reviewing should be a continuous process, arising out of day-to-day activities, supplemented by meetings and giving and receiving feedback.

What do you consider to be the skills required for a good reviewer?

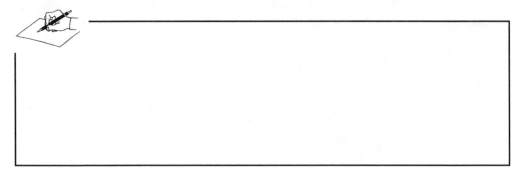

The skills needed are:

- monitoring — to satisfy yourself that effective and regular reviews are being carried out

- analysis — to verify that all the objectives, including any revisions, suit the overall plan

- judgement — to ensure that objectives remain consistent, following any amendments.

Reviewing should be thorough and systematic. However the review process should not be bureaucratic and written paperwork should be kept to the minimum.

So how do all these 'contributing' group methods work?

Of course, they all work differently, but we feel that the central characteristic of all of them is that they:

- **rely on the learners' knowledge and experience.**

Where the group is primarily 'spectating', the trainer or the film or the demonstrator is the source of all the knowledge. In 'contributors' group learning for much of the time the learners learn from each other, or from themselves, because they are encouraged to take a fresh look at the implications of their own knowledge, experience or attitudes.

We're talking about:

- learner-centred training

with the trainer as facilitator making it easy for people to learn for themselves.

We see the process skills of questioning and reviewing as vital to this approach. Both these skills are intended to help learners to draw out of the lessons what they and the other members of the group have experienced, said or done. Contributors' group learning without making use of these skills is like pushing a car with the engine switched off. It requires a lot of effort, doesn't get very far, and ignores the most powerful source of progress.

Summary

Chapter 2 has dealt with group training. We have shown the difference between learning by 'spectating' and learning by 'contributing'.

We have described three types of 'spectating' learning:

- lectures

- video and films
- demonstrations

and considered where these methods could be most useful.

We then went on to consider the more exciting style of 'contributing' learning. We divided this section into two groups:

1. Those which are dependent on the interaction between people:

    - brainstorming
    - discussions
    - role-play

    and

2. Those where people learn primarily from the activity and only independently from each other:

    - case studies
    - exercises
    - simulations.

The advantages and limitations of each method were explored and the types of learning objections were given.

Finally we considered two process skills which are crucial to the success of 'contributing' group learning:

- questioning
- reviewing.

Assignment 1:

Plan out a script for a training session using one or more of the techniques described in this chapter and design any materials it may need.

Assignment 2:

Pick just one item of your training provision (planned or current) and then examine it in the light of our table on the following page.

The table, as you'll see, looks at how good group-based training — by which we mean a broad and appropriate mix of the various techniques described in this chapter — will sit with the four areas described in chapter 1.

There are tick boxes for you to use. The more ticks you get the more we would recommend you select group-based training in your situation.

If you find the top two boxes full of ticks, but the bottom two empty — then group-based training is necessary — but you need to change the situations in the bottom boxes before you can implement it.

Subject Matter

Group-based training will be effective if the subject matter:

- ☐ is complex and requires analysis
- ☐ involves applied knowledge
- ☐ involves skills (simulations and demonstrations)
- ☐ requires learners to compare experiences

- ☐ is debatable
- ☐ involves decision-making and problem-solving
- ☐ involves interpersonal skills
- ☐ involves discussion of various options

Learners

Group-based training will be effective if the learners:

- ☐ are activists
- ☐ are reflectors, but outgoing enough to share their insights with the group
- ☐ are theorists, but willing to cast sidelights on the subject under discussion

- ☐ are in one central location
- ☐ are six or more in number

Training Resources

Group-based training will be effective if your training team:

- ☐ has adequate access to suitable premises
- ☐ has suitable equipment
- ☐ has the skills to use the equipment
- ☐ has qualified trainers or access to them
- ☐ has interpersonal skills

- ☐ has process skills

Organizational Expectations

Group-based training will be effective if your organization:

- ☐ is prepared to make a sizeable commitment to training
- ☐ has special interest in professional and management training
- ☐ is confident in the ability of the training function

- ☐ is committed to group development

Chapter 3

Side-by-Side Training Explained

This chapter deals with side-by-side training under its various names. Those names we shall mention in particular are coaching and on-the-job training (OJT) which we shall study in some detail.

Using the principles discussed, you will see what you need to do to prepare for and implement OJT.

Next, you will consider the process of teaching major tasks. And finally, you will look at suitable approaches in your organization.

By the time you have finished this chapter you should be able to:

- list the strengths and weaknesses of side-by-side training

- state the key principles of OJT

- develop a system for OJT and be able to describe the basic steps for setting up this system

- ensure effective teaching and be able to identify the basic steps for an instructor

- improve the supervision of training practice

- decide, using your knowledge of all the above points, whether OJT is suitable for your situation.

Defining Side-by-Side Training

Side-by-side training is one of the most natural training processes in the world. Every time we say to a less experienced friend, colleague or member of the family, 'Let me give you a hand' or 'Have you tried it this way?', we're instinctively offering side-by-side training.

We probably wouldn't call it that. Even in a more formal, commercial training context, the process is called a variety of different things:

- side-by-side training
- coaching
- one-to-one training
- on-the-job training (OJT)
- 'sitting next to Nellie'
- supervised practice.

The process we're talking about is a method of individual training in which the trainer encourages the learner to acquire new skills and habits in a practical way by practising them under the trainer's guidance and supervision.

Most usually, side-by-side training takes place in the workplace, with a more experienced or senior colleague carrying out the function of trainer.

Think about your own experience and the definitions we have given above concerning this training process. List what you see as the strengths and weaknesses of side-by-side training.

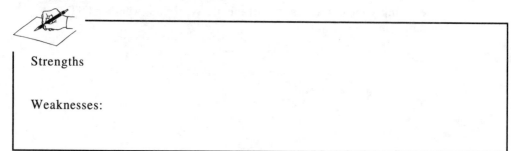

Strengths

Weaknesses:

Now compare your ideas with ours:

Advantages of side-by-side training:

- learnt in the workplace therefore practical and realistic
- taught by someone who knows the job from experience
- the job is seen in the proper context
- skills taught are real and up-to-date
- requires no special resources.

Limitations of side-by-side training:

- person responsible for training may have neither the knowledge nor the skills to train
- person responsible for training may only know how **he or she does the job**, not how it **should be done**
- workplace is often noisy, frenzied and distracting — a bad place to learn.

We expect you'll have spotted two fundamental contradictions between our earlier statement that side-by-side training was natural and instinctive and the weaknesses we've just listed. We may have an instinct to help other people, but most often that instinct leads us to tell the other person precisely what to do, or even to do it for them. And if we do that, they won't learn. So, we feel it's important to make these two points very clear:

- side-by-side training is a complex skill which needs to be learnt like any other
- an 'expert' in the skill may be too competent to teach the basics to a beginner.

There is a common core of philosophy and activity which runs through all side-by-side training. It tends to be workplace-based. It tends to be based on a one-to-one relationship. It tends to eschew formal instruction. The commonest manifestations of side-by-side training are probably on-the-job training, which we shall look at in detail next, and coaching, which shares the same principles, but needs a separate gloss.

On-the-Job Training (OJT)

On-the-job training is in danger of turning into merely a 'training substitute'. That is, it could be believed that if you dump an unskilled and inexperienced trainee next to a skilled and experienced 'Nellie', all the skills and experience will seep into the trainee, as if by osmosis. Nothing of the kind. OJT should be as structured as any other form of training if it is going to be effective and relevant to the job the individual is going to do. That implies:

- **a break-down of the job to be learned**
- **converting the job elements into objectives**
- **testing knowledge and skills against these objectives.**

The results of the testing will give, of course, the relevant contents of any OJT.

We shall take each of these three stages in turn.

Job analysis

Job analysis is a hierarchical process, top down, to find out exactly the elements of any job. For instance, let us take, as an example, a baker's job and see how that can be analysed:

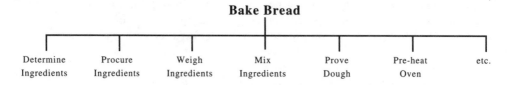

In some cases, the second-level job elements have to be analysed further: common sense will tell you when you have got to a single, integral and intelligible job element.

There are several ways a job analysis like this can be effected. Try:

- talking to employees who can do the job already

- observing proficient employees doing the job
- reading training/technical manuals which could give the information required
- learning to do the job yourself.

Writing objectives

For training purposes, job elements should be turned into learning objectives. This way, each trainee will know exactly what is expected of him or her. To know exactly what is required presupposes some qualities that the objectives must have. These qualities have been stated and related in generally consistent terms over the years. In one form or another, each objective must state:

- what is to be done. The statement should be simple and unambiguous, contain an active verb and an object. For instance: '**set** (active verb) **temperature** (object)'
- how it is to be done. That is, any conditions, tools, environmental considerations that are necessary: 'set temperature to **gas mark 6** (the 'how')
- to what standard it is to be done. The standard could be qualitative ('consistently, appropriately, accurately') or quantitative ('within ten minutes, to a weight of 50 gms'): 'set temperature to gas mark 6 **15 minutes before baking**' (the standard).

Assignment:

Research a single, simple job being regularly performed in your organization.

Either: *find out how that job has been analysed and what objectives have been applied to the job elements*

or: *analyse the job into elements yourself and apply objectives.*

This process will ensure that your OJT is targeted and relevant to the organization's and individual's needs, and cuts the 'hit or miss' element that can creep into OJT.

Testing knowledge and skills

The job has been analysed and the job elements have been turned into learning objectives. You now need to know which objectives your trainees can fulfil and which they cannot. Those they cannot fulfil become their training regime in OJT.

There are various ways of assessing a trainee's competence against objectives, ranging from:

- performance judged against criteria
- competence marked off against a sliding scale (say 1-5)
- a simple 'fully competent/needs training' classification.

The trainee and the on-the-job trainer should both have a current copy of the 'live' objectives — that is, those that are being worked on at any one time. Also, to keep those objectives 'live', they should be revisited and updated regularly — say once a quarter.

So far, then, we have identified three principles underlying the practice of OJT. To restate them, those principles are:

- proper analysis of the job
- conversion of job elements to learning objectives
- matching individuals' competence against those objectives to see where the training need lies.

Having identified these principles, you should now look at a credible process for developing OJT.

Developing an OJT System — the Process

The following training management process for OJT is based on one which was developed originally for the American army, but is now regularly applied within commercial, industrial and service organizations. We shall take each stage one by one, with a brief explanation.

1. Compile a Training Database

The database should include:

- job analyses, learning objectives and current individual training requirements (see above)
- a list of jobs prioritized according to their importance to the organization. This will help you decide on a sequence for your OJT provision and a full training schedule.

2. Develop and Implement a Plan to Manage OJT

The prioritized training schedule has been established. You also need to find out and document:

- who will be needed to give the training (and what implications that has for others)
- who will pick up the jobs the trainee will leave for the duration of the training
- how long jobs will take to complete during the training period

and to:

- inform everyone in the system (trainer, trainee, substitutes, etc.) of their role
- inform everyone of what tasks are to be trained and when
- inform everyone of the arrangements made to accommodate the training.

3. Select the Personnel for Training

You already know who needs training in what, and you have a prioritized list of training needs. But you cannot assume that everybody who needs OJT can be released immediately. Ask those who have knowledge of the individuals and their work — supervisors, foremen, etc. — to select both trainees and trainers for the OJT programme.

4. Co-ordinate Support Resources

It will be necessary to identify any material resources (for instance, hardware and software) the OJT will require and make sure they are available with a minimum of disruption.

5. Provide the Training

Select employees with proven competence in the job to be trained to do the training.

6. Evaluate the Training

Evaluation should be based on at least three key questions:

- have trainees gained the required competence?
- have the appropriate competences been trained?
- is there an increased sense of job satisfaction and motivation in the workforce?

The first point can be simply evaluated if good objectives were set in the first place. As to point two — whether the appropriate skills have been trained — there will be certain success indicators to show that, including:

- improved production
- fewer accidents
- less down-time
- favourable comments from customers
- increased business.

The third, about morale in general, could be measured against:

- less absenteeism
- better timekeeping
- more and better contributions to quality circles.

Evaluation against objectives is constant, irrespective of what subject you're covering or where you work. This contrasts sharply with success indicators for the competences being trained in and the amount of increase in motivation, which vary from organization to organization.

7. Document Training Progress

Trainee and trainer should continuously exchange feedback on progress. This is an essential but generally informal element of OJT.

More formal records should also be kept of trainee progress against objectives, so that these can be passed on to management. Ideally, the trainees should keep a record of their own progress against objectives and maintain it, regularly. They then can pass on copies of their personal records to the trainer who will know (a) what the trainees **have** achieved and (b) what they **think** they've achieved.

8. Monitor the Training

Again this is continuous. The training manager will need constant feedback on:

- individual progress against objectives (see above)
- difficulties with personnel resources or environment caused by the training initiative
- any other indicators of success or failure which manifest themselves within the organization.

With this information, the training manager can keep adjusting or fine tuning the OJT which is taking place to ensure it continues to meet the needs of the organization and the individuals involved in the training.

How to be an On-the-job Trainer

As On-the-job trainers are chosen for their competence at a job, and only secondarily for their ability to train, there is some basic theory and practice of training they need to understand if they are to be effective in their role.

How the Learner Learns

First of all, the trainer should understand something of the process by which the trainee learns. Detailed educational psychology will not apply, as in most OJT circumstances the trainee will be asked to become competent at some discrete and relatively straightforward tasks. So, what will be happening in the trainee's head? Something like this:

1. Second-hand experience of the task (hearing instructions, witnessing practice)

    ↓

2. Hands-on experience of the task.

    ↓

3. Give and receive feedback on competence.

    ↓

4. Trainee adjusts performance accordingly.

    ↓

5. Continuous and correct practice.

    ↓

6. Second-hand experience of **another** job.

    ↓

Etc.

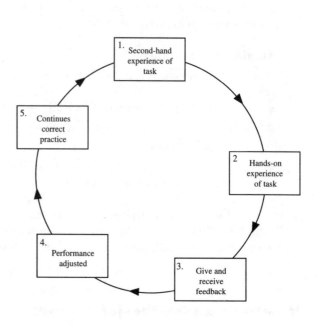

Checklist for OJ Trainers

Now you understand something of the learning process, there are some tips which will help OJ trainers to make the learning happen. They should:

1. Find out what the individual's training needs are: which objectives the trainee has not yet met.

2. Check they have the right environment and resources with which to train.

3. Explain their objectives, why they are training, and keep the trainee at ease.

4. Show rather than tell, explain the 'why', and get feedback by asking open questions.

5. Know their subject, keep the order of events logical and their language simple.

6. Coach — and not drive the trainee at an inappropriate pace.

7. Keep the training active and the trainee working.

8. Make sure the trainees get to practise what has been demonstrated — **immediately**!

9. Back off as the trainee becomes more competent — but remain as support for the trainee, and identify others who will perform a similar support function.

How to Give Feedback

The giving and receiving of continuous feedback has been reiterated throughout this section of the book. There are several simple but valuable points which OJT trainers should remember about giving feedback. They should:

1. Give feedback the moment it is required — not save feedback for 'feedback sessions'. The feedback must be associated immediately with the task.

2. Make the feedback logical, specific, unambiguous and easy to understand. If it **can be** misunderstood, it **will be** misunderstood.

3. Give positive rather than negative feedback where possible, and never be judgemental.

4. Demonstrate, and give experience of, what happens when a job is done:

    *   properly
    *   wrongly.

    Success is the greatest teacher. The trainee golfer will always remember the grip that improves the swing.

5. Maintain the flow of feedback after the training is complete, so that the trainee has the opportunity to reinforce all that has been learned.

In the light of all you have read about OJT, think about any OJT you have organized, seen organized, or had organized for you. Write a line or two on each of the following.

- How was the training planned?

- How was the training implemented?

- How was it monitored?

- How was it evaluated?

- What differences were there between what has been described above and what happened?

- What advantages/disadvantages did these differences bring?

Finally, as promised, a brief gloss on coaching.

Coaching

Coaching is about facilitating the trainee's own learning. The coach will not teach or tell, but create the conditions in which the trainee can discover and learn. So the coach is not a tutor, but an available resource. The coach will need, in particular, the skills to guide and counsel, leaving the learner to deduce and conclude.

A good coach will need some knowledge of the job and of coaching skills. Very often, non-trainers in the workplace are successfully trained and prepared to take on this role.

Summary

In Chapter 3, you started with the various aspects of side-by-side training.

You then considered the strengths and weaknesses of this type of training.

Next, we turned to on-the-job training and explored in depth the use of this technique. We explored three major components of OJT:

- job analysis
- writing objectives and
- testing knowledge and skills.

We also described how to develop a system for OJT using eight basic steps, broadly adapted from those used by the US Army. This system has direct application to industrial, commercial and service situations. These were:

1. compile a training database
2. develop and implement a plan to manage OJT
3. select the personnel for the training

4. co-ordinate support resources

5. provide the training

6. evaluate the training

7. document the training progress

8. monitor the training.

This was followed by:

- nine basic steps the instructor can take to ensure effective OJT
- five points for providing feedback.

Finally, we completed the analysis of circumstances where side-by-side training was a suitable approach in your organization.

Assignment 1:

Prepare materials and/or workshops which will train individuals to improve their own OJT performance. Include the main points of this chapter, but made specific to your own situation.

Assignment 2:

Pick one item of your training provision (planned or current) and then examine it in the light of our table on the following page.

The table, as you'll see, looks at how good on-the-job training — by which we mean a sound application of the technique described in this chapter — will sit with the four areas described in Chapter 1.

There are tick-boxes for you to use. The more ticks you get, the more we would recommend you select on-the-job training in your situation.

If you find the top two boxes full of ticks, but the bottom two empty — then OJT is necessary but you will need to change the situation in the bottom boxes before you can implement it.

Subject Matter

OJT will be effective if the subject matter:

- ☐ is practical
- ☐ involves a real skill which is currently used
- ☐ is best understood in its proper context
- ☐ is part of the daily routine

- ☐ can be divided into sub-tasks or elements

Learners

OJT will be effective if the learners:

- ☐ are practical
- ☐ are keen to get hands-on experience of the task
- ☐ are open to constructive criticism and correction

- ☐ need a one-to-one relationship

Training Resources

OJT will be effective if:

- ☐ the people responsible for the training have the necessary skills for the job being trained in
- ☐ the people responsible for the training have the necessary **training** skills
- ☐ the 'trainer' is not too 'expert'
- ☐ the 'trainer' is trained to coach

- ☐ the training department can complete the database, plans and analysis required before training starts
- ☐ the training department can coordinate and support the training
- ☐ the training department can document progress and monitor the training scheme

Organizational Expectations

OJT will be effective if the organization:

- ☐ has the experience within itself to do the job being trained for
- ☐ respects the input of the training function into OJT

Text-Based Open Learning Explained

There has been a huge growth in open learning in recent years and the quality of the material available is improving all the time.

We start this chapter by spending a fair amount of time defining open learning both from a theoretical and from a practical point of view. This part of the chapter is applicable to both text-based methods that we will be discussing here and to the technology-based methods which are to be discussed in Chapter 5.

At the end of this chapter you will be able to:

- define open learning

- distinguish open and closed styles of learning

- identify the benefits of open learning material

- describe the four essential components of a successful open learning system: effective materials, efficient administration, trainer support, and opportunities to practise or discuss

- list the key differences between text-based open learning and more technical approaches, eg, computer-based training, compact discs and interactive video

- clarify the circumstances in which text-based open learning is relevant to you.

Defining Open Learning

Open learning has become more effective as a training method over the last ten years, as trainers have learnt more about it and the quality of material has improved.

At the same time though, many organizations have tried open learning, got their fingers burnt and pulled out as a result. We believe that, in many cases, this has been because trainers and managers assumed that all other forms of training have suddenly become redundant and that open learning can be introduced as a replacement, with little if any support, regardless of the subject or the learner. That's why we are spending time here at the beginning **defining** open learning in some detail.

How Can Learning be Described as Open or Closed?

Open learning frees learners from many of the limitations and restrictions of conventional training and education.

What are these limitations? We can list them by answering five short questions:

- **Who will learn?**
  In conventional or closed learning schemes, there are often entry qualifications and conditions which close learning to certain people.

- **What?**
  Once a course is chosen, the precise choice of topic is restricted.

- **When?**
  The pace, times and length of study are usually dictated to the learner by someone else. Typically, the pace of learning is geared to the 'average' trainee, making it too fast for some and boringly slow for others.

- **Where?**
  Conventional learning happens at a given place, sometimes at a centre at an inconvenient distance from the learner's home or workplace.

- **How?**
  Resources, methods and assessment are decided by someone else.

By definition, therefore, conventional training and education set up several barriers to learning. Only the keenest are likely to stick it out.

Open learning doesn't necessarily give the learner the opportunity to make **all** these decisions for themselves. But it does make it possible for the trainer or manager to choose **how open** their approach to training will be, without being limited by the determining factors of a conventional approach.

That means we can draw up a spectrum of openness. Think about the training that normally takes place in your organization. Look at our matrix here and decide where this training would fit.

	Closed								Open
Who?									
What?									
When?									
Where?									
How?									

What are the implications of your training's degree of openness?
Which issues would you want to make more open and how would you do it?
Write your answers to these questions below.

Of course, we don't know your organization. But if you run a mainly closed style of training, you might like to think about some of the following implications.

Implications of a closed style of training are:

- people are 'sent' for training. Some may be unwilling, others who want training may be excluded. This has implications for motivation, for career development and for the skills and knowledge available to the organization

- closed training is disruptive. The need to conform to set times and locations may well not suit the demands of the work. Travelling time, in particular, is unproductive

- learning styles are ignored. Learners are given no choice of **how they learn**. Training may be ineffective if training methods and learning styles don't match.

We can now provide a theoretical definition of open learning:

- **open learning is an approach which takes place in a way and at a time, place and pace convenient to the learner.**

We've called this a 'theoretical' definition to help you recognize a potential trap. Some trainers have assumed that, because open learners are supposed to make all the decisions about their learning, they shouldn't expect any help, support or guidance. Many open learning schemes have failed precisely because of this assumption. So we need to make it clear that open learning can only be as open as the support system will allow. Indeed, your organization may deliberately choose to close parts of the scheme; for example, by only making training available in one medium, say text; or by specifying what training certain people can receive.

How far learning can be made truly 'open' will depend to a large extent on the resources an organization is prepared to make available. CBT, for example, demands far more in the way of resources than text-based open learning. You'll see what we mean by this concept of limited openness as we move on.

What are the Benefits of Open Learning Materials?

We hope that we've said enough so far to give you an insight into the benefits of open learning.

Now we want to look at these benefits more particularly from the different points of view of:

- the learner
- the trainer
- the organization or sponsor.

Can you identify any of these benefits? Write your suggestions here.

Here are our lists.

Benefits of open learning to learners:

1. They are freed from conventional time plans and centres. They choose to study at their own time, place and pace.

2. Objectives enable learners to skim over things they can already do, then study carefully when something new comes up.

3. Activities, checks and self-assessments let learners know how well they are progressing, praise correct responses and guide the learners if they've made any errors — in the security of privacy.

4. Regular summaries enable learners to review or revise something they studied some time ago.

5. Good materials are stimulating and friendly! The learner *wants* to carry on.

6. **Learners have more control of the learning itself. A good package will help them to develop study skills useful in any future context, and give each one the feeling: 'I'm getting there myself'.**

Benefits to the trainers:

1. Better able to satisfy the needs of people who are slower, faster or more or less skilled than the average learner.

2. Freed from many of the repetitious or routine 'information-giving' tasks of training.

3. Can expand the options and content of training, and train many more than in a conventional training course.

4. May be able to start new learners studying at any time.

5. Can use face-to-face sessions to concentrate on practical applications and individual learning needs or problems.

6. **Each trainer becomes a more flexible facilitator and tutor, with work which is more diverse and interesting — and more useful to the organization!**

Benefits to the organization or sponsor:

All those we've mentioned! Plus:

1. Standardization of high quality training throughout a company, without the costs of face-to-face training 'off-the-job'.
2. Minimizes the geographical barriers for national or large regional companies.
3. Shorter lead times to respond to training needs as they arise.
4. More rapid updating is possible.
5. For many smaller companies open learning material can be the first real chance to make essential training cost-effective.

How 'Open' Should Open Learning Be?

There are four essential components to a successful open learning system. These are:

- effective materials
- efficient administration
- trainer support
- opportunities to practise or discuss.

Think about these four components for a few moments from your own practical standpoint.

You should be able to recognize that each of these components imposes some limits on openness.

Effective Materials

Providing **effective materials** involves finding relevant commercial packages, or writing or tailoring your own. All of these can be costly and time-consuming. So the variety of subject matter and delivery media you can offer will be limited by cost and availability. A learner who wants to know more about a personal hobby or interest, or who wants to develop a skill which is not relevant to the current job, will be a lower priority than someone else with a training need which directly affects performance. Delivery media may also have cost and availability implications. There is a wide range of text-based open learning available, and new technical programmes are constantly being produced. Some material is of high quality, other material less so. So there are constraints here too.

Whatever the type of open learning, it is the materials or resources which take on the main task of 'teaching'. They are not at all like conventional texts or handbooks. Even if you flip through a study booklet very quickly, you should notice there's a lot for the learner to *do*. Activities are scattered through all the pages. You should find clear objectives and regular summaries. This guide provides a good example.

There'll be some sort of regular *self-assessment questions*. You'll find suitable *responses* to the questions too, written in a friendly style, and space for the learner to write in the booklet.

A variety of media may be used in open learning. We've already mentioned printed study books: they are the most often used medium. But computers and interactive video are becoming more popular, as well as video and audio cassettes, and practical kits. There are a number of integrated, multimedia open learning packs on the market.

Efficient Administration

The need to provide **efficient administration** also limits what you can do. You may need to keep down the learner population by setting entry requirements, simply so that your administration meets budget constraints. You may also need to set start and finish dates for packages, so that assessments happen in manageable blocks, rather than in a totally random fashion. So freedom of time and pace may be limited.

Any training system includes administration and management, and open learning systems are no different. The sort needed depends on the scale and nature of the open learning system that you implement. It may include despatch of materials and regular, quick turnaround of assignments, or procedures for final assessment.

As with any training, all these components will need constant monitoring and evaluation. Indeed the more learners there are taking your provision and the greater their distance from you, the more rigorous your monitoring needs to be.

Trainer Support

Trainer support is essential, as we have said. If your learners choose to take openness of access to an extreme, for example by learning at 3 o'clock in the morning on holiday on a Greek island, you are unlikely to be able to provide effective support. As a result, either the openness or the support are bound to suffer.

The trainer

Despite what you may be thinking, the trainer is the key to the success of open learning. The trainer's role has changed — to one that is more lively and challenging. You can be free from all the repetitive aspects of information transfer. You can devote your time to the real individual needs of your learners, providing guidance and counselling to each one.

The trainer becomes more of a tutor or facilitator. This may include being a tutor *at a distance from the learner,* marking assignments, and possibly talking through problems on the phone. But face-to-face sessions are important too.

Opportunities to Practise or Discuss

The need for opportunities to practise or discuss the material has implications for how open the choice of place and time can be. Practice sessions and tutorials are difficult to arrange on an individual basis, so they need to take place at preset times, in a suitable venue. Once again, learners' freedom is restricted.

Practical work and face-to-face sessions

Many types of training demand practical work with equipment or facilities that can't be included in individual packs. With open learning, the learner can be directed out of the study material to undertake some practical work-related activities. Alternatively, these can be provided at special face-to-face training sessions; one of the lessons of open learning has been that even distance learners profit from some face-to-face learning:

- live sessions are useful for practical work, group discussion and analysis — anything in which learners must *participate* together

- for lots of people who are 'distance' learners, human support — from the trainer as well as other learners — is especially important. Learning totally on your own is a lonely business.

The best starting point for anyone who's thinking of including open learning in their standard training provision is to plan to use such materials for what the materials can do best, and save human resources for the things that need human skills.

We've summarized these four key components of an open learning system below.

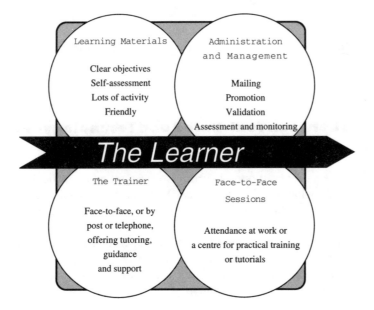

Now pause for a moment after this summary of open learning and work out for yourself why you consider it to be an effective training method. What is the greatest value of open learning?

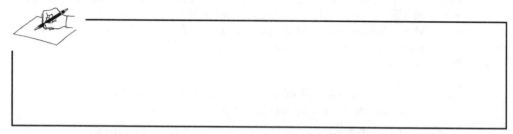

Please remember: the great value of open learning is *not* that it provides one more strict system. Its value lies in its flexibility to adapt to the needs of different learners, clients and organizations.

Two Different Types of Open Learning

Now we are going to look at the two different types of open learning: *text-based* and *technology-based,* to compare them and note the key differences between them.

Differences Between Text-based and Technology-based Open Learning

Most of what we've said about open learning so far applies regardless of the delivery method you use. So what are the differences between text-based and technology-based open learning methods? We've listed the key differences below:

- text is the most easily accessible. Working through a text-based package requires the ability to read and write, nothing more. Technology-based training requires access to some comparatively complex and expensive equipment

- text is not very interactive. Although text-based open learning involves questions and activities, the writer can only guess the learner's answers. The newer technologies can enable students to link data, information and ideas and can provide an interactive learning situation where learners can become actively engaged in the learning process

- text is ideal for knowledge, less appropriate for active skills. Legislation, procedures, facts and figures are ideal subjects for text-based packages. The more practical the skill, the less able the printed page is to handle it. Interactive skills, like handling sales objections or interviewing, work much better either with role plays or interactive video. Of course this is where text-based material can be backed-up with practical sessions or tutorials

- text needs a significant level of trainer support. We've already mentioned the need for trainer support of all kinds of open learning. Text, in particular, because it's a lonely medium, needs a skilled trainer or tutor to motivate, monitor and give feedback

- text is relatively inexpensive to update. Updating text-based open learning requires either the issue of correction slips or complete reprinting (a slightly more expensive but more satisfactory option). Amendments to technology-based training prove difficult and expensive.

We hope that what we've said so far has fired your enthusiasm for open learning. We also hope it's given some practical guidance as to what does and doesn't work in open learning.

Summary

Chapter 4 has shown you the value of open learning, and in particular the value of text-based methods.

We started by defining open learning both from a theoretical and a practical viewpoint.

Then we introduced the idea of a spectrum of openness and asked you to think about some of the implications for your own organization.

The benefits of open learning materials were then introduced from the different points of view of:

- the learner
- the trainer
- the organization or sponsor.

The limits of openness were then discussed under the headings of four essential components of successful open learning:

- effective materials
- efficient administration
- trainer support
- opportunities to practise or discuss.

These components were summarized in a diagram of an open learning system.

Next we discussed the four key differences between text-based and technology-based open learning.

Finally we asked you to assess the criteria of the circumstances in which you would use text-based open learning in your organization.

Assignment 1:

Using the knowledge gained from this chapter define the role of a trainer within your organization in arranging and supervising a particular text-based open learning unit.

Match your definition against your team's current competences and arrange for development if necessary.

Assignment 2:

Pick one item of your training provision (planned or current) and then examine it in the light of our table on the following page.

The table, as you'll see, looks at how good text-based open learning — by which we mean such that conforms to the description in this chapter — will sit with the four areas described in Chapter 1.

There are tick-boxes for you to use. The more ticks you get, the more we would recommend you select text-based open learning in your situation.

If you find the top two boxes full of ticks, but the bottom two empty, then text-based open learning is necessary, but you will need to change the situation in the bottom boxes before you can implement it.

Subject Matter	*Text-based open learning will be effective if the subject matter:*
☐ is knowledge-based ☐ provides background knowledge for application elsewhere ☐ is intended to impact on attitude ☐ is general **or** specific	

Learners	*Text-based open learning will be effective if the learners:*
☐ are theorists or reflectors ☐ are comfortable with the printed word ☐ are dispersed or centrally located ☐ have the same basic learning needs	

Training Resources	*Text-based open learning will be effective if:*
☐ commercial material can be bought (for low numbers of learners) **or** there is expertise available to the team to develop customized materials ☐ materials are chosen or developed carefully, with an eye to relevance and language level	☐ sufficient time is allowed to set it up properly ☐ human support is available ☐ an administration system is set up

Organizational Expectations	*Text-based open learning will be effective if the organization:*
☐ is prepared to let trainees set time aside at the workplace ☐ encourages line managers to be sympathetic ☐ can justify purchase or development costs	☐ is keen on self-assessment **and** external assessment ☐ needs consistent message to be put across in its training.

Chapter 5

Technology-Based Training Explained

High technology approaches to training are sophisticated forms of open learning. The learners learn at their own pace, in their own time and when and where they are motivated. So much of what has been said in Chapter 4 on text-based open learning can be applied to this section as well.

What is important to recognize is that computer-based training, interactive video and the newer interactive technologies are still not the answer to every training need.

In this chapter we are going to look at some of the developments in technology for training purposes. In particular we will describe these four types:

- Computer-based Training (CBT)
- Interactive Video (IV) and the newer interactive learning media
- Compact Disc-Read Only Memory (CD-ROM)
- Compact Disc Interactive (CD-i).

By the time you have finished this chapter you will be able to:

- distinguish between the different types of technology
- list their advantages and disadvantages
- describe linear and branching programmes
- comprehend the future challenge of technology
- select the most suitable technology for your use.

Development of Technology

Now let's have a look at the development of training technology over the years.

Early *Computer-based training* (CBT) was primarily text based, and involved little real interaction with the user. As computer technology advanced computerized graphics, animation and sound were incorporated allowing increased learner interaction.

The introduction of *Interactive video* (IV) coupled the computer with a video disc player. This powerful alliance of video and computer technologies broadened the scope of subject areas that could effectively be tackled with CBT, and further enhanced learner interaction and control.

Today we are at last being given a glimpse of the true potential of the computer in the learning environment. *Interactive multimedia* (IM), the latest CBT advancement, combines the traditional elements of CBT with full motion video, digital sound, and photograph quality images. This harnessed to the power of modern computers provides exciting new ways of exploring, analysing and communicating information, and provides for full learner interaction.

The *compact disc* (CD) has made a tremendous impact over the last ten years in audio reproduction. It is now an emerging force in computer technology due to its ability to store vast quantities of data, such as is necessary for multimedia. The influence of CD on CBT is likely to be as great as in the audio world.

CD technology is also at the heart of *Compact Disc Interactive* (CD-i). This represents an attempt to move the boundaries of CBT away from the desk top PC, and to provide IM through a simple console attached to a television set, much like a conventional video cassette player.

Four Types of Technology

1 Computer-based Training (CBT)

This is a generic term which covers a large number of approaches to training. It allows the learner to interact with a training programme through the use of a computer. The training material can take the form of electronic text, graphics, sound, and latterly multimedia.

Conventional CBT programmes are written onto standard floppy discs and loaded onto a hard disc or computer network, giving the learner flexible access to the training they require.

2 Interactive Video (IV)

Interactive video combines high quality laser disc video images with the traditional elements and control of conventional CBT. Programmes are written onto laser discs, and accessed through a special player interfaced with a PC. The laser technology makes the cost of developing tailor-made software somewhat prohibitive, but the format is well established and there are plenty of high quality generic products available.

3 Compact Disc — Read Only Memory (CD-ROM)

In this system training programmes are written onto CDs which, due to their large storage capacity, support multimedia. This highly interactive, and user friendly form of CBT is accessed through a CD-ROM drive connected to a PC. The power of the PC can be harnessed to enhance the features of the system. As the CD-ROM discs are read-only format, which does not permit the recording of any data, the addition of an Electronic Performance Support System (EPSS), which records the achievements and progress of learners using the training programmes onto the PC, provides the trainer with an all-round training and evaluation system.

4. Compact Disc — Interactive (CD-i)

Compact Disc-Interactive embraces all of the features of the CD-ROM system in a single console that can be used with a conventional television set. Learner interactivity is controlled through a simple hand held remote control unit comprising a joystick or mouse and several directional touch keys. It is the ideal medium for training in the home, with small groups in a seminar situation, or for those who fight shy of computer technology. CD-i machines are relatively inexpensive and double up as a home entertainment system for games, photo and music CDs. However unlike the CD-ROM, as there is no interaction with a PC, the CD-i system does not currently allow for the addition of EPSS.

Now you should be able to set out your own ideas concerning the advantages and limitations of technology-based training.

- Advantages

- Limitations

Here are our answers.

Advantages of Technology-based Training:

- high levels of motivation through the sheer novelty value of the media
- interactivity means the training can closely match the needs of the learner

- the medium is relevant to a wide spectrum of knowledge and skills
- gives immediate and detailed feedback to learner
- reduces the need for tutor support
- cheap to maintain.

Limitations:

- high initial costs (becomes more cost-effective with numbers, geographical spread, or regularity of use)
- long lead time for initial production.

Types of Programme Used

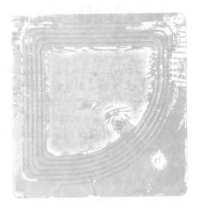

Broadly there are two kinds of learning programme:

- linear programmes, and
- branching programmes.

Linear Programmes

A linear programme presents learning in small steps or frames. Each frame calls for the learner to respond to a simple question. By 'cueing' the learner before each question, the programme ensures that as many as 90 per cent of the responses are right. It will respond to an incorrect response by routing the learner back to an appropriate earlier frame. For short, simple learning sequences the linear programme can be quite effective. But it has severe limitations on learner activity. Once the topic has been selected, the learner has few choices beyond answering the questions or opting out. Mistakes or wrong answers are not given any special treatment, so the individual's interests or learning needs are ignored.

Branching Programmes

These programmes offer many more frames and much more learner choice than linear ones do. They offer the full complexity of sophisticated multiple choice, or even open-ended questions. The learner who gives an incorrect answer will enter a special 'branch' which provides remedial learning or a fresh learning approach. In the same way, 'branches' can be offered to meet a range of starting levels or special interests in the topic.

Can you see how the amount of branching that any programme offers has to have some limitation? The limitation is in human time and money!

The Challenge of New Technology

The challenge now for the producers of technology is to make interactive multimedia as desirable and affordable as TV and the telephone. Trainers have to make creative and innovative use of the technology. We have to learn to creatively develop the communications potential that the current technologies offer. The future belongs to those who can determine how to make this new technology meet the needs of the learners.

Many organizations choose to ignore interactive multimedia (IM) because they perceive it as expensive. But it is important to remember that IM can be:

- low cost

    and

- fast.

The hardware, once purchased, can be put to many different uses, for example, a video camera can be used to record original material so that trainers and learners can create their own productions.

Summary

In this chapter we have taken a brief look at technology-based learning.

You noted that many of the ideas expressed in Chapter 4 on text-based open learning apply here as well.

You looked at the development of technology and then defined four particular areas:

- Computer-based Training (CBT)
- Interactive Video (IV)

then the newer technologies:

- Compact Disc — Read Only Memory (CD-ROM)
- Compact Disc-Interactive (CD-I).

Then you considered the advantages of technology-based training.

Two types of programme were next outlined:

- linear programmes, and
- branching programmes.

Finally, you took a brief look at the challenge of new technology and how you could fit technology into your own training methods.

Assignment 1:

1. *List the different forms of technology you would like to have available for your training.*

2. *Plan a resource library that you could build up, starting with a few priority programmes and then looking forward to future developments.*

Assignment 2:

Pick one item of your training provision (planned or current) and then examine it in the light of our table on the following page.

The table, as you'll see, looks at how good technology-based training — by which we mean practices in keeping with the principles outlined in this chapter — will sit with the four areas described in Chapter 1.

There are tick-boxes for you to use. The more ticks you get, the more we should recommend you select technology-based training for your situation.

If you find the top two boxes full of ticks, but the bottom two empty, then technology-based training is necessary, but you will need to change the situation in the bottom boxes before you can implement it.

Subject Matter	*Technology-based training will be effective if the subject matter:*
☐ deals with knowledge ☐ deals with applied knowledge using the high-tech medium (eg banking) ☐ involves the learner in decision-making ☐ leads to one right answer, or	☐ creates situations where there are several possible correct answers

Learners	*Technology-based training will be effective if the learners:*
☐ find other training methods boring and predictable ☐ have a wide range of abilities and experience ☐ are sympathetic to technology, even though they need not be experienced in its use	☐ are able to access the hardware and software ☐ are numerous (if a package is to be developed)

Training Resources	*Technology-based training will be effective if:*
☐ you have experts available should you decide to develop your own training, or ☐ you have time available to shop around, should you decide to buy an off-the-shelf product ☐ you allow time to test the training	☐ your training department has the hardware and software needed for training packages, or ☐ on-line hardware has the capacity to run your training package (in terms of time and compatibility)

Organizational Expectations	*Technology-based training will be effective if the organization:*
☐ can fund the purchase/development of packages ☐ is sure of the innovative ability of the training function ☐ can provide the hardware/software capacity you need	

Chapter 6

Discovery Learning Explained

Discovery learning is very much in line with the principle of 'learner-centred' training we've been following throughout this book.

In this chapter we will consider the three main approaches to discovery learning:

- designing a case study
- setting a real-life business problem
- action learning.

We will look at the general activities involved in each of these approaches. As usual we will describe the advantages and disadvantages of this learning method. Finally we will consider the circumstances suitable for you to use discovery learning.

At the end of this chapter you will be able to:

- define discovery learning
- list the three main approaches
- discuss action learning in detail based on four general activities relevant to self-development
- select the best techniques for your own use.

Defining Discovery Learning

Discovery learning is probably the most natural of all forms of learning, so it's surprising that so few organizations structure it into their overall training strategy. Perhaps that's because, although it's natural, it requires a lot of thought and preparation to make it succeed. In essence, discovery learning involves setting up one or more activities, exercises or projects which provide opportunities to learn and then encourage the learners to draw their own lessons and conclusions from the experience.

Three Approaches

There are three main approaches to discovery learning. We will start with the simplest and move on to the most complex.

The Simplest Approach to Discovery Learning (Case Studies)

This is a matter of designing or selecting a case study or physical activity and providing the learners with access to:

- human
- physical or
- paper resources

which they can use to solve the problems set by the exercise. In this form, discovery learning uses the techniques we've already explained in the second part of Chapter 2 in this book under the description of **case-studies** and **simulations**.

A More Complex Approach (Real-life Business Problems)

This second approach sets a group of learners a real-life business problem. The question to be answered is this: 'If you were responsible for this aspect of the business, what would you do about it?'. In this case, the learners will need to investigate the situation, identify shortfalls and then have access to resources which will allow them to tackle the shortfalls.

The problem set does not need to be serious, or current, nor does it necessarily need a solution. What is important is that it does, or did, exist and that relevant data should be available. Tutors need to be available to facilitate the analysis and problem-solving aspects of the exercise. It adds some spice to the training if managers who are, or were, involved with the problem are available to comment on the solutions.

The Most Complex Approach (Action Learning)

Action learning extends and builds on the principles of problem-solving we've already described. With this approach, a group of participants tackle a real-life problem, in a real work situation. If you think that sounds like what we all do every day, you'd be right. But action learning is more than mere learning by doing. It harnesses the full learning potential of the whole group. For example, learners would work with a number of other people with complementary responsibilities. The learners would meet together regularly. The problem each individual would tackle would be a current and difficult one in your organization, in need of a solution. The group would each bring their own problem with them. As a group they would review the issues, exchange ideas on how to approach them, then go back to work to implement the solutions. They would meet regularly to report back on progress, snags and successes. Your role as trainer would be to **facilitate** these training sessions, arranging times, means, resources and materials.

Action learning can be extended as far as you and your organization choose. Each person in the group might come from a different discipline within an organization, or even from different organizations. This would give the learner fresh insights into problems from different perspectives and experiences. They might even agree to **swap jobs with someone else in the set for a while**, so everyone really gets to experience a range of problems. The task of the group would be to share ideas, solutions and so on.

Action learning is based on four general activities:

- applying a scientific method
- pursuing a rational problem and decision
- exchanging advice and criticism
- learning new behaviour.

All these activities are relevant to the self-development of anyone whose work involves decision making or problem-solving.

Advantages:

- what is learnt is retained in the learner's mind
- the learner identifies his or her own learning strategies and can apply them on future occasions
- relationships are reinforced
- learning is very **effective**
- learning is **immediate**, done **in context**, so no transfer of skills is needed.

Limitations:

One of the main limitations of this method is that it will usually take a long time to prepare. Also it takes longer as a process than, for example, a straight lecture. But it is well worth while persuading the sponsor to give extra time for this type of learning.

When to Use Discovery Learning

The more complex a form of discovery learning you adopt, the more preparation and organization it requires. So you need to be selective in the people you invite to experience it and to recognize that there are only limited circumstances to which it can be applied. You should also appreciate that not all organizations would be able or willing to support discovery learning as a training method. Nevertheless, for the right people and in the right circumstances, it can be a very powerful learning vehicle.

Summary

In this chapter you have looked at discovery learning in some detail. We have defined discovery learning and considered three approaches to its use:

1. the simplest approach, using the same techniques as case studies and simulations

2. a more complex approach setting a group of learners a real-life business problem

3. action learning, the most complex approach.

We have discussed action learning, based on four general activities:

*   applying a scientific method

*   pursuing a rational problem and decision

*   exchanging advice and criticism

*   learning new behaviour.

You then looked at the effectiveness of this method and considered its advantages and limitations.

Our next chapter will provide you with a quick way of comparing each training method.

Assignment 1:

Choose an 'action learning' situation. Plan it, and justify its use to your superior.

Assignment 2:

Pick one item of your training provision (planned or current) and then examine it in the light of our table on the following page.

The table, as you'll see, looks at how good discovery learning — by which we mean practices in keeping with the principles outlined in this chapter — will sit with the four areas described in Chapter 1.

There are tick-boxes for you to use. The more ticks you get, the more we should recommend you select discovery learning for your situation.

If you find the top two boxes full of ticks, but the bottom two empty, then discovery learning is necessary, but you will need to change the situation in the bottom boxes before you can implement it.

Subject Matter

Discovery learning is effective if the subject matter:

☐ is complex

☐ has no right or wrong answers

☐ involves problem-solving and decision making

☐ involves interpersonal relations

☐ involves self-awareness

Learners

Discovery learning is effective if the learners are:

☐ fairly senior

☐ able to cope with the threat of the unknown

☐ experienced

☐ practical learners

☐ individuals or small groups

Training Resources

Discovery learning is effective if:

☐ you are able to undertake considerable planning, preparation and arranging

☐ you have skilled facilitators

☐ the organization can give full support in terms of data input

Organizational Expectations

Discovery learning is effective if the organization:

☐ supports non-traditional training methods

☐ is committed to individual self-development

☐ is keen to see **overall** job performance improve

Chapter 7

The Final Choice

If you've worked through all the chapters in this book, and completed the assignments at the end of each chapter, it's possible that you already have a clear indication of which training method is going to be appropriate for a given element of your training provisions.

But it's possible, too, that you're going to find yourself in a dilemma. The indicators may not give a clear signal one way or another. And the more items you examine, the more likely it is that you're going to come across a certain proportion which could be delivered through one of several training methods.

So, how do you choose? And even if the indicators do point to one method — is it a good idea to commit yourself without making sure? And how do you make sure?

By the time you've worked through this chapter you will be able to:

- explain the importance of testing new training methods
- describe a sequence of actions you should take to ensure testing is accurate
- devise a strategy for the selection of training methods in your organization.

Since this last point is the main purpose of this book, we suggest you move on now to tackle the rest of this chapter without delay.

Making Sure

Whether the signals from your basic indicators focus on one method or more than one, eventually you're going to have to choose.

Think for a while now about that choice: what are the best consequences of it going right? What are the worst consequences of it going wrong? And what are the implications for you in either case? It's worth taking five or more minutes to think long and hard about those questions, and writing the answers in this box.

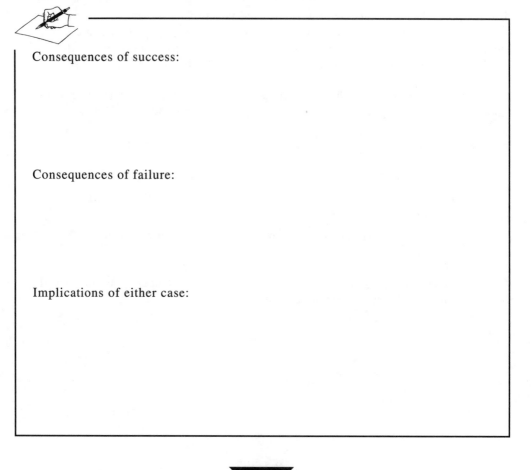

Consequences of success:

Consequences of failure:

Implications of either case:

We imagine that your consequences of success included items like these:

- individual trainees' targets being met or exceeded
- individual careers being developed
- individuals being empowered and motivated to learn
- group targets being met or exceeded
- an improvement in your organization's performance
- plaudits being revealed by the trainers
- an increase in confidence in the training function
- more training resources allocated next year
- job security for yourself and your team.

And, not to labour the point, the consequences of failure would be exactly the opposite.

The implications in either case are that the stakes are high; there are a lot of people with a lot riding on your choice, so it had better be right. And it follows from this that you should make every possible effort to make sure it is right before you start.

Once you've arrived at this (inescapable) conclusion, other spin-off benefits become apparent:

- if the organization needs proof that the new training initiative is going to work, then the more you've done to ensure success, the more you'll be able to show to your decision makers to put their minds at ease
- if you're interested in fine-tuning your skills in selecting training methods (and you are), then you will also be interested in developing efficient, inexpensive and reliable ways of checking that your selection is correct.

Everything we have said under the title making sure has been focused on ensuring the success of new initiatives, but, of course, it applies equally to existing training which you are seeking to update or amend. Making sure is a key part of your job — but how do you do it?

Developmental Testing

The answer in the vast majority of cases is to arrange a developmental test. These can be cost-effective, efficient, quick and can provide you with reliable, rough and ready information on which to base your final selection.

The developmental test must be run as a project, because there is a sequence of actions to be gone through if you are to be sure that the test itself is a success. We have seen developmental tests unworthy of the name: situations where a trainer has acquired a training disc from somewhere, sat down in front of a screen, run through a sample of the program, and on the strength of that 'development' has ordered thousands of pounds' worth of training material. This source is not recommended. A more methodical approach will be more reliable.

Step 1: Fix the Timescales

If you're in a situation where a training programme of some sort has to go live next week, and you don't know which method you're going to use yet, then you're in trouble. Either you've mismanaged the selection process or your organization hasn't a clue about what the training function's job actually is. If the latter is the case, then you should address the problem at a strategic level: implement some training immediately to ease the pressure you're under, but make it a priority to educate the organization about the nature of the job. If you're in trouble because you haven't left enough time yourself, well, this section of this book will ensure it never happens again.

You have to ensure that there is sufficient time before full implementation to developmentally test at least one and maybe more methods. This implies a need to plan. The developmental test is not just a rubber-stamp exercise to be completed a fortnight prior to going live; you have to allow yourself time for a complete rethink; time to set up something different if the test shows your method is inappropriate.

You'll understand more about how much time to leave when you've seen what's involved in each subsequent step.

Step 2: Choose your Samples

What do you need samples of if a pilot test is to work? Write your answer in here.

You need samples of:

- the material or the method you're testing
- the learners
- (possibly) the training team.

When identifying samples you should remember that you're trying to gain information about a small part of something which will enable you to build up a picture of the whole. In other words, your samples must be representative.

You may have to draw materials and method samples from more than one place; if your proposed training method involves, say, some open learning followed by role-plays in a one-to-one situation, then your sample should reflect this.

Your learner samples should be drawn from a cross-section of potential trainees, bearing in mind age, experience, educational background and, of course, the job they do.

If your training is to be delivered by a range of trainers — perhaps even by line managers drafted in to do a little specific coaching, then you should include a cross-section of these individuals as well.

Step 3: Carry out the Test

We recommend that you tell the people involved that they are involved in a developmental test, if they don't know already; it's just a way of being even more certain of their co-operation.

The circumstances of the developmental test should mimic the real-life circumstances as nearly as possible. There is little point in testing, say, an open learning text designed to be used as and when pressure of work permits by asking the trainee to down tools for a week and concentrate on the learning; you will only get a false impression of its effectiveness.

The major difference between the developmental test and real life should be that the trainees (and trainers as well) are asked to comment on the learning experience as it happens — so that, for example, immediately a point has been learned, the trainees are debriefed so that you know how they found the experience: could it be improved? How? Was it too easy? Too hard? Just right? Was it relevant? Appropriate? Why? And similarly the trainers are asked for their comments on how things seem to have gone.

Of course you have to be careful not to drown the learning experience with too many questions too often, but even so, you should try to gain some feedback during or immediately after the training.

Step 4: Collect the Results

When the sample of the training is completed you should gather in the feedback the trainees and trainers have been providing during the test. This will give you valuable information about whether the training is going to motivate people or not — an important element in your decision to go for full-scale implementation or not.

Step 5: Select the Training Method

Equipped with your results you can probably select your training method with confidence. You figured you were on the right lines after your use of the assessment grids, and the developmental test has confirmed it.

It is possible that the test will show you which way you need to be going.

The most likely outcome is that the pilot will show you not only that you've selected the right method — it will also show you ways of incorporating improvements into it even at this very early stage.

Evaluation

Evaluation of training, at its best, is an ongoing thing, so it's likely that you will be constantly evaluating your current training provision. This evaluation will reveal whether or not the training is working, and if it isn't, then clearly there's a problem for you to address. And the solution could be a change of method — in guidelines in this book.

You can read more about evaluation in *Evaluating Training* — book 7 in this series, which also gives a slightly different perspective on developmental testing.

Summary

In this final chapter of this book, you saw that it is vitally important for your selection of training methods to be correct; there are many people who have a vested interest in its success: your learners, everyone connected with the organization, and not least you yourself.

To be sure you've selected the correct method, you should test it — and a developmental test will only succeed if you run it as a project with these five steps:

1. fix the timescales

2. choose your samples

3. carry out the pilot

4. collect the results

5. select the training method.

Finally we reminded you that while the five-stage process outlined above is suitable for new training initiatives, further evaluation of your current training will occasionally throw up items of training which are failing — and the solution may in these cases be to select new methods using exactly the same process.

Assignment:

Take an item of your planned training provision (or a planned upgrade of your current training provision) for which you have not made a final decision as to the best method to use.

Use the grids at the end of each chapter in this book to identify the method most likely to succeed and test it using the five step plan outlined in this final chapter. Keep careful records of all your actions and bind them together in a file.

This file will serve as evidence of your experience in selecting training methods; within your organization it will be a permanent record and justification of your ultimate choice.

Conclusion

By choosing your methods in a disciplined way you will be able to achieve the following:

- specify your training needs
- select the most appropriate method
- identify the areas and situations where each method is likely to succeed
- evaluate your choice of methods critically
- make informed judgements about the potentially most successful methods
- provide efficient resources, with less chance of costly errors
- create the most effective learning situations
- satisfy your trainees
- provide an overall improvement in your organization's performance.

Further Reading

Training Methods that Work
Lois Hart Kogan Page 1992

Teaching Through Projects
Jane Henry Kogan Page 1993

Teaching with Audio in Open and Distance Learning
Derek Rowntree Kogan Page 1994

The Trainer's Desk Reference
Geoffrey Moss Kogan Page 1993